ACTORS SPEAKING

Actors Speaking

EDITED BY LYN HAILL

INTRODUCTION BY PETER GILL

OBERON BOOKS
LONDON

First published in 2007 by Oberon Books Ltd.
521 Caledonian Road, London N7 9RH
Tel: +44 (0) 20 7607 3637 / Fax: +44 (0) 20 7607 3629
e-mail: info@oberonbooks.com
www.oberonbooks.com

A catalogue record for this book is available from the British Library.

PB ISBN: 978-1-84002-776-1

Contents

Acknowledgements

The National Theatre Studio, in the Cut in Waterloo, is the NT's engine room. It provides an environment where writers, actors and artists of all kinds can explore, experiment and devise new work, free from the pressure of public performance.

The people conducting these interviews, singly or in pairs, were: Philip Brook, John Burgess, Phillip Joseph, Michael Maloney, Angela Morant, John Price and Robert Swann. With the exception of Michael Hordern and Margaret Tyzack, who were interviewed in 1988, the conversations took place in 1986.

Thanks to John Burgess, Gavin Clarke of the NT Archive, Jonathan Croall, Lucy Davies, John Goodwin, Peter Hall, Sue Higginson, Paul Miller, Stephen Unwin, and to Richard Mangan of the Mander and Mitchenson Theatre Collection.

Lyn Haill
Head of Publications, National Theatre
www.nationaltheatre.org.uk

SPEAK TO ME

An Introduction by Peter Gill

When I set up the National Theatre Studio in 1984, the development and analysis of acting was a central part of the work, so that, along with commissioning writers, developing directors and designers, investigating non-text-based work, and producing work for the main house, the practice and analysis of acting skills seemed an essential part of any programme of work that was in part concerned with process. Among all the classes for actors of voice and movement, of improvisation and analysis, the separate issue of the speaking of text, old and new, was an important part of our work, and for a particular reason. Young actors were under attack at the time for their apparent lack of skill at handling text. The view held by many was that although they were a very talented generation, and were on the whole more edgy and real than their seniors, capable of playing a wide range of parts and with unusual access to feeling, they lacked the skill with the speaking required, particularly of difficult texts and more particularly with speaking Shakespeare. The criticism was general but not entirely accurate. In the matter of dialect for example, they were infinitely more adept than their older colleagues. But although there was a thinly veiled class element to all this, the criticism was not entirely without justification. It seemed that the essential connection between acting and speaking was being lost, and that this was not a kind of parental disapproval about good taste on the part of older colleagues, nor a disdain by the young for a received pronunciation which was seen as middle class and uncool. There was a lack of feeling for speech itself, for the manner in which writers had written, even in dialect, even in their own. The celebration of language was gone. There was a plausible speaking of Shakespeare from the universities but without the real bite required.

What had led to this situation? There was much speculation. Was it the fault of schooling? Did child-centred creativity leave out learning to speak other people's words? Was there a lack of experience of speaking aloud for its own sake? Was it the lack of opportunity to listen to anything rhetorical and effective in the way of public communication – as there had once been from pulpit and political platform? Was there lack of access to old skills? Was it new working patterns in television and films? Were the young feeling the lack of weekly rep, which had been so useful to older actors? Was it acting with different needs? Or was it that speaking itself was irrelevant, that speech had been outgunned by other means of expression in a time of cynical populism? Did this generation find Shakespeare as difficult as their elders had found Chaucer? Did they find too that any attempt at making the speaking clear and expressive was not acknowledged, and that the fashion for over-demonstrative, conceptual productions, while failing to mask the problem, seemed for some to be a solution to it?

To my generation of actors, a good deal older than those under scrutiny, any idea of an applied technique had seemed old fashioned. Elocution spoke of class, style of artificiality. But now it seemed that the erotics of speaking, the celebration of language, had been forgotten in the pursuit of other concerns. For us, speaking and acting were still vitally linked, although not as they had once been. We had learned much by osmosis, as it were, by being on stage with older actors, listening. Recollected sensing is a vital part of the acting skill.

There was, I believe, a modern movement of acting in – or rather peculiar to – Britain, at around the beginning of the last century, which had as much to do with speaking and its connection to acting as anything else. This movement was linked to an idea of textual supremacy, of writing and acting being central to the theatrical form, in its concern with the importance of speaking, and its insistence on the musical needs of the text. It was different from the movement elsewhere in Europe. It shared in most of the aspirations of Stanislavsky and the French realists but always in the context of how the play was written, what was its tone.

The Vedrenne-Barker seasons staged at the Royal Court Theatre from 1904 to 1907 are a good place to start this discussion, although the genesis of those seasons lies much earlier. Perhaps it is William Poel (whose productions of Shakespeare made such an impact and have had such an influence on all subsequent ones) who was the great precursor to the Court Theatre seasons as far as acting was concerned. Harley Granville Barker played Edward II for Poel in 1903 and was influenced by his insistence on the actor's valuing the text and its integrity, on speaking that was swift, clear and musical, and playing that supported this. The aim of Barker and his colleagues at the Court was to present new plays in a more coherent way, one that was quite at variance with the commercial theatre that then obtained and with the pre-eminence of the actor manager. What Barker and people like him were in contention with was an outmoded, irrelevant, sensational theatre, which peddled a fodder of melodrama, romances, and farces – all vehicles for stars. Reform of the old school of acting was needed, particularly of its speaking, its phoniness and its bombast. They wanted a modern approach to both modern plays and old ones. Lewis Casson, who had acted for Barker and for William Poel, says in an interview given for the BBC when he was 90, and recently discovered by Jonathan Croall, 'I saw how Barker was applying to modern plays the method of Poel for Shakespearean speech, of analyzing the text and interpreting it through definite, stylised music, chosen to produce the greatest emotional and intelligent interpretation of the actual thought and emotion.' Sybil Thorndike, Casson's wife, herself a product of this school, says in the same broadcast, 'People were thinking it was the most natural speech they'd ever heard,' and later, of Casson directed by Barker, 'His speech sounded the most natural, ordinary, everyday speech and yet every thought was so clear – meticulously clear – that you were inside his mind immediately and inside his personality.'

The acting at the Court Theatre during that period was noted for its excellence, and since some of the actors were also in other companies while they played matinees at the Court, this was demonstrable. Max Beerbohm, in his review of *The Voysey Inheritance* in 1905, notes: 'People often ask, quite innocently, with a genuine desire for information, why the acting at the Court Theatre seems so infinitely better than in so many other theatres where the same mimes are to be seen. I should have thought that the reasons were obvious: that the mimes at the Court are very carefully stage managed [*directed*], every one of them being kept in such relation to his fellows as that demanded by the relation in which the various parts stand to one another – no mime getting more, or less, of a chance than the playwright intended him to have.'

The existing theatre implicitly criticised by the 1904 Court was lacking in intellectual rigour and any desire to represent life as it was. There had been few plays of significance since Sheridan: there had been

Boucicault, Bulwer-Lytton and Thomas Robertson, and more recently Pinero and Alfred Sutro, and there had been Wilde. The Romantic poets had produced pale copies of Shakespeare, which were thought unperformable. The novelists had other concerns: the women novelists were bound by convention, as far as the theatre was concerned, and thought the whole business had no place in the intellectual life of the country. The person who best exemplified any seriousness at this time was Henry Irving who, with actor-managers before and after him, was a beacon in a dark world. Irving was essentially a Victorian, concerned with making the theatre a profession for gentlemen. He wanted to rid the theatre of its old immoral reputation and actors of their reputation for profligacy and dissipation, and to raise the standards of the profession above the image created in Dickens' Vincent Crummles, the actor-manager in *Nicholas Nickleby*. Yet Irving produced few plays of importance outside Shakespeare, no modern writer of significance, and nothing that was intellectually challenging.

But there was another dimension to the British theatre. Theodor Fontane, the German novelist, author of *Effi Briest* (the Effi of *Krapp's Last Tape*), was in England in 1860 to review the theatre for a German paper. He often found the more refined and advanced German theatre disadvantaged by the vitality, the *joie de vivre* he found in the English theatre of Astley's circus, the Shakespeare on horseback, the Surrey theatre, the 'penny gaffs', and the emerging music halls.

In *Trelawny of the Wells*, Pinero found something of that vitality, backstage. In his thinly veiled portrait of Squire Bancroft, his wife Marie Wilton and their protégé Tom Robertson, Pinero bears witness to the charm and personality of the old actors and to a world that had no place for Gradgrind and Mrs Proudie. It is to actors like Bancroft that we owe any continuance of playing Shakespeare; it was they who developed the younger actors, and to them fell the cost of keeping up standards. Older actors are always deep in the affections of their younger colleagues, and so it was then. Edward Gordon Craig acted with Irving and was always devoted to him, as was Meyerhold to Stanislavsky, for whom he had played Konstantin in the first production of *The Seagull*.

The Vedrenne-Barker seasons were notable not only for the variety and dynamism of the programme, but for the standard of the acting and the productions, which were welcomed by a public hungry for serious theatre. One of their chief concerns was to put to bed the sound and the fury of the older actors, no matter how charming and alluring they were, and replace it with something more graceful and natural. There were others in the struggle too: J T Grein, Elizabeth Robins and William Archer for example, who championed the cause of Ibsen in England; the Stage Society, which brought the great forgotten plays to the stage; and Miss Horniman, who funded the Abbey Theatre in Dublin and founded a new repertory theatre in Manchester.

But the desire for change came not only from the more serious side of the theatre; there was a revolution too in the commercial theatre, where notably Gerald du Maurier and Seymour Hicks developed a style, particularly in light comedy, of an apparently effortless charm – light, understated, expressive, witty – which had a great effect on the acting that came after them and may be why all the great English actors of the 20th century were consummate comedians. Du Maurier in particular was influential because, although he never played the classics, he did play in contemporary dramas where he used his effortless technique to great effect, doing as much with his back and his cigarette case as anything else. It was this school of performing that helped to modernise American acting when it was seen there. Many of the new European developments, however, had no influence in Britain at all. This was principally because ours was a commercial theatre circumscribed by political censorship and, although our apparent insularity is sometimes a front for longing, philistinism and diffidence played their part too. But there were some to whom the acting in the experimental European theatre seemed bogus in an English context. The acting of Nikolai Cherkasov, who played Ivan the Terrible in Eisenstein's films, was expressive but seemed no different from the old style here: its vitality was envied but not copied. Rather like Robert Helpmann's performance in the film *Chitty Chitty Bang Bang*: ideal for pantomime, but not thought *à propos* in a theatre that has always been concerned with the poetry of observed reality.

In 1945, after the second world war, the time came for another shift in the movement towards a serious theatre in Britain. Much of what had seemed exemplary before, in particular the kind of acting that was admired, was more and more being put to the service of everything that was moribund and class-bound. Much of what Barker had pioneered at the Court and later at the Savoy, and what the Abbey Theatre in Dublin and the repertory movement in England had stood for, had had very little effect outside its small sphere of influence. There were valiant fighters on the fringe of things, in the so-called Little Theatres. There was Lilian Baylis and Barry Jackson, there were enlightened managers like Bronson Albery and later Hugh Beaumont. Theodor Komisarjevsky and Michel St Denis were great influences when they settled here, and there were the writers – Somerset Maugham, Githa Sowerby, John Galsworthy, James Bridie, J B Priestley, Noël Coward, Terence Rattigan, Rodney Ackland – all hampered by the twin impediments of commercialism and the Lord Chamberlain. Many of them, and the directors too, succumbed to a reactionary code, shying away from what was important in the European theatre under cover of thinking it pretentious and humourless.

Two of the theatre's most important visionaries had also jumped ship. Edward Gordon Craig had left England early on. He had never taken any practical part in the struggle here; his ideas were influential only in their European context, and many thought him a dilettante. Harley Granville Barker, who had certainly been part of the struggle, left the theatre after his second marriage to take up the life of a literary gentleman in Paris, and was thought to be the lost leader who had betrayed his disciples. Class issues had become paramount and there wasn't a moral aesthetic to address them. Examination of British films about the war, and who the makers thought had won it, is testament to that. The directorial theatre of Europe seemed an empty flourish and appeared to have served its purpose (even if unfortunately not here), and anyway didn't satisfy British empiric spirit. The boulevard theatre in France certainly didn't solve the problem. The answer was not a smart, ultimately cowardly, commercial theatre nor a flimsy art theatre, but something different, something which incorporated the ideas of Barker and the others into a new vision. Even the humour, the lightness of touch brought by du Maurier to the West End stage seemed reactionary and to have lost its sting; many of the class attitudes of the actors on stage were risible, particularly the generalised 'off' accents used to suggest life below stairs. The soldiers' vote which brought Labour to power in the 1945 general election meant, however, that even the British theatre would eventually have to change, stumbling along as it then was under the burden of commercial imperative and political censorship (which would take until 1968 to reform). British theatre looked once again to its writers and to a new directorial and managerial energy, taking its cue from the reformed expressionism of the Berliner Ensemble; the actors looked towards America and its revisiting of the ideas of Stanislavsky.

The trajectory of the modern theatre has been greatly influenced by the visions of Ibsen and Wagner, which were about different types of seriousness. Ibsen banished a certain kind of poetic diction from the theatre in order to dramatise the tragedy of the middle classes; Wagner envisioned a total theatre of all the arts combined for a more symbolic purpose. This trajectory had largely been energised by the directors who emerged in the wake of Ibsen and Wagner. There had, of course, always been a director figure – someone who oversaw the production, a job done by different people at different times. The modern director came in large measure from two strands of theatre. In the European theatre, the position emerged out of dramaturgy, full of ideas and fancies; in Britain from stage management, more intuitive and practical. In Europe, the authorial side of the directorial movement found funds; here, not at all. And there have also been two ways of looking at the serious theatre. One is to find ways to bring the various strands of art and of life into a kind of poetic harmony, often in sequential narrative; the other seeks to mirror a fractured world in a more separated, less coherent way. The tools for making both these approaches work are still part of our working practice, whether the epic one of Craig and Meyerhold or the more human one of Stanislavsky and Barker. The second still saw the actor and writer as central; the first disputed the position of both. In each case the director is seen as pre-eminent.

Was there an actor who epitomised the modern movement of Barker and Poel? There were many, but the one who seemed to crystallise the synthesis of acting and speaking was a tall, plain, charismatic genius who was a Pimlico milliner until she played Cressida for Poel in 1912 and who became an actress when she was 29.

I first saw Edith Evans as Katherine of Aragon in the all-star production of *Henry VIII*, mounted by Michael Benthall to celebrate the completion of his five-year Folio plan at the Old Vic in 1958, with Harry Andrews as Henry, John Gielgud as Wolsey, and Judi Dench as Anne Boleyn. My memory of the production is only of Edith Evans, whose performance remains for me a touchstone of all that is impressive in the kind of theatre I have been talking about. In Katherine's 46-line speech (Act II, Scene 4), beginning, 'Sir, I desire you do me right and justice,' she played one long intention of entreaty, an arc of pure action, while by means of her consummate control she took us down every avenue of thought and feeling to be found in the text, never failing to sustain the principal action. There was a perfectly judged natural flow of feeling expressed in her physical life and her exquisite speech. She was at once a political victim, a wife, a daughter, a princess, and a queen, creating her part in the dialectic of the scene exactly and making for Henry a perfect contrary. There was a dissolution of ego and a complete embodiment of the text shining through a personality of great luminosity. Evans was a phenomenon: a great actor while not a great box office draw, admired by her peers while not being particularly easy or clubbable. Many of her performances were landmarks. Her Millamant and Mrs Sullen for Nigel Playfair at the Lyric, Hammersmith, helped to bring the Restoration dramatists back into play. A supreme comedian with total command of the audience, whom she never allowed to control things, she was uninterested in chasing laughs. She played a wide range of class but was unable to play a character she couldn't sympathise with, and so restricted herself, often being called on to make the preposterous credible.

And who of the new wave emerging in the fifties and sixties epitomised the acting of that time? I can think of two who best showed what was new and what was different about the actors of my generation. And this may be because they made a particular impression on me. One of them, Nicol Williamson, was a tall, rangy, laconic, unusual, Midland Scot with yellowish hair, a nasal delivery and not much physical charm. The other, Victor Henry, a vivid, short-sighted, auburn-haired Yorkshire scrap from Leeds. Both had electric, if not always pleasant, personalities; both brought a burning life to what they did and an uncompromising commitment to the moment. Theirs was acting outside any exercise of technique or good taste, and they, while not in the first wave of the new acting, epitomise for me how seismic the change was. Neither of them was glamorous like some of their contemporaries; in that they were very like Edith Evans. Like her, they were committed to the text, though not to the same extent as she and without her artistry. There was an unrehearsed urgency to what they did, as if it was a matter of life and death. Both were variable, both strangely competent, both charismatic and eminently suited to the writing of the time, particularly to John Osborne's unhappy invective. Victor Henry was the definitive Jimmy Porter in Anthony Page's revival of *Look Back in Anger* in 1968 at the Royal Court, capturing the pain and the rage and the folly of the man. Nicol Williamson gave a landmark performance of the middle-aged hero in the premiere of Osborne's *Inadmissible Evidence* (1964), again directed by Page. Both took those characters' narcissism onto a different level of anguished elegy. Victor Henry didn't play much of the classical repertoire, nor did he find playing the upper classes easy. Neither actor was a natural for Frederick Lonsdale. But at the Royal Court, as Tim, the Cambridge student, in his duffel coat and spectacles in William Gaskill's production of *A Chaste Maid in Cheapside* (1966), and as Tom in a revival of *The Knack* (1966), Henry was charming and funny. He was full of sweetness as Sparky in *Serjeant Musgrave's Dance* (1965), and in the D H Lawrence plays (1967) full of romance, heartfelt, overflowing with feeling and sensibility. Williamson played a great deal of Shakespeare and was the Hamlet of that time (Round House 1969). Though vocally unpleasing, it was a marvellously phrased and spoken performance of such speed and attack that it seemed as if Shakespeare was writing in a vivid vernacular. Both brought to their acting the flickering of life. They were neither of them vain actors, both sure of their talents, and seemed only complete in performance. Both were hard-working in the rehearsal room (Victor couldn't work much outside it). I didn't find him difficult to direct, even though he was a handful. I did find Williamson hard work but then he set the bar very high for himself. They neither of them thought themselves director-proof or created their parts outside the rehearsal room, as Laurence Olivier would. They gave the lie to any idea that acting at this level can be willed by a director or cooked in some way. Actors like these can be cast, bullied, cajoled, shaped – in short directed. They cannot be manufactured. Directors can find them, nurture them, put up with them, try to change them, teach them even, but there is a kind of acting that is beyond manufacture in production, no matter how flashy the *mise en scène* or how holy the intention. These two were not as attractive as older actors like Albert Finney and Peter O'Toole. They were more like rock singers of the Janis Joplin kind. This was brought home to me when I met Victor Henry after I had been reading Antonin Artaud's *The Theatre and its Double* and realised that he was the actor Artaud was asking for, but outside any manufactured directorial agenda. Both Henry and Williamson seemed troubled men. It was commonly thought at the time that Victor might die young, that his ungovernable nature might kill him The irony is that he was knocked down by a car and died after surviving for years in a vegetative state. Williamson found things increasingly problematic and performing more and more stressful. He had a higher public profile than Henry and, had he been more sensible, he too would be teaching at Hogwarts and making spells in middle earth. He hardly works on the stage now and lives in America. To Henry, a career plan was what twats had. Though both these actors spoke well they were part of a movement that inevitably took the younger actors to where they found themselves under attack.

What we did at the Studio was no more than to raise the issue of speaking and provide access to classes for the NT company to address the subject. Apart from the regular voice work for the NT actors, classes in textual analysis, in-house productions of classical plays, and workshops of all sorts, I tried sometimes to be more interventionist. In 1985, for instance, fifteen young black actors were resident at the Studio to study Shakespeare for three months, culminating in a performance of *Macbeth* played in dialect at the Cottesloe theatre. I sometimes, too, invited older actors in to teach. Among these was Gwen Ffrangcon-Davies who, aged 98, took a group of young actresses through the major speeches and scenes of Juliet, a part she had first encountered as a girl, when her father, the baritone David Ffrangcon-Davies, introduced her to Ellen Terry. As a part of this initiative, in 1986, I had the idea of sending a group of younger actors out to interview older ones about their attitudes to text. All these great actors, except for one, are dead now. I knew some of them and I admired them all, and their kindness and hospitality to young actors was very touching. I chose these actors because I thought that they made a template of all that I admired in speaking by older colleagues.

There were thirteen of them that we asked. Gwen Ffrangcon-Davies and Athene Seyler were the oldest, being born in 1891 and 1889 respectively. They had been in at the beginning of the modern movement; the others had grown out of it. Some of them had international reputations;

all of them were admired by their peers and there was an amazing breadth to their work. Alec Guinness and Rex Harrison were stars of international standing. Harry Andrews and Michael Hordern were more local stars. Robert Stephens and Margaret Tyzack were of a different generation from the others. Fabia Drake and Patricia Hayes were leading ladies of seemingly opposite poles: Fabia Drake appeared more establishment and Patricia Hayes, who had had a classical training, had supported all the great comedians of the time. Madoline Thomas and Gabrielle Day were exquisite character actresses of a peculiarly British kind. John Gielgud, thinking that the aide to the interview which I had sent him was a questionnaire, filled it in with his familiar, beautiful handwriting.

What do they tell us? Well, actors are not great analysts of acting and, if they are, they usually give it up, as Barker and Stanislavsky did. Our actors were rather surprised at being asked about speaking, the importance of which they took as a given, yet it transpires they had all thought about it and worked at it. They certainly didn't think good speaking would come from enthusiasm. What they were most concerned with was being real, being truthful. They were anxious that speaking wasn't seen as some drawing-room niceness. That it was vital, not fancy. In that, they were children of the Barker ideal.

Any conclusions I have been able to reach about speaking have come from listening to actors like these. It seems to me that good speaking requires first of all the development of an ear. An ear for what the writer has written – its cadence, its tone – and a felt need to find the technical means to express this, so that it appears as if these are the speaker's own words. A feeling for the integrity of language for its own sake is required, an identification and celebration of the word, and – most importantly – the word's place in the phrase. Phrasing is all, and phrasing forward towards the stop. To be reliant on punctuation only as far as is necessary for clarity and musicality is important, acknowledging the stop and never over-marking the commas. Producing only the voice required by the writing and the situation – nothing more and nothing less; recognising that the same rules apply to writing of every period. Of course classical writers are harder to speak, for obvious reasons, and can be daunting to some people. They involve more agility and control and breath. Shakespeare is hard for the young and untutored. The classical allusion, the extended fancy, some of the syntax, the use of antithesis, can be overwhelming, as they can be in other classical writers whose writing often seems formal and unnatural. It needs confidence and work. As for the connection between acting and speaking: why, it is the same thing. The action is encoded in the way something has been written. Acting and speaking are bound together. Listening to the tone will unlock the intention, help to activate a line, as much as any method, and will be more accurate in discovering what the intention actually is. There can be a kind of censorship in denying the way in which a line has been written, reducing it to what can often be an arbitrary decision about action and intention, when it is only in the writing that you get any information about what these really are.

To talk about something as protean as acting in terms of dates can never be precise. The school of acting initiated at the beginning of the last century must have had its inception earlier and was further developed over the next fifty or sixty years. That which apparently brought about the theatrical revolution of 1956 must have had its beginnings before that, too, and is still developing, just as the Method used by Marlon Brando and his generation in America hasn't been superseded but refined since then.

The pool of actors has widened and is just as talented but acting is not regarded as it once was, and the wider racial mix has not yet been given a chance to show where it might take us. When it does, it certainly won't be by means of government targets. But the charge about speaking remains, as the drama school curriculums whirl about on the periphery of things and those in charge resolutely refuse to address this elephant in their room. The young actors have all the temperament and personality to play the classical parts but are not trained now to play any writer before Ibsen, while directors and reviewers are seduced by an idea of directorial spin and ignore the problem. It is not sensible to expect that actors should turn up to the first day of rehearsal of any play written before 1900 and pick up the necessary tricks in a few weeks by means of a generalised approach, a reach-me-down, post-Stanislavsky, one-intention-fits-all business. Learning to speak well is a personal matter, too, and if what it entails is not understood and embraced by the actor, then no amount of external prompting will do. Barker and du Maurier were actors. A change in acting has, as it were, to be a grass-roots thing. But the working patterns of actors have so changed that that will be very difficult to achieve. Many young actors are content to start and finish their careers in television and many of the more successful find a greater need to hang out in Hollywood, on the off-chance of a lucrative offer, than to prepare themselves to play Congreve, on the off-chance that someone might produce him. There have always been actors fit for different things, specialists in differing ways. It may be that certain of the current demands on an actor may narrow his range. The difficulty of playing old texts has been ignored for too long and it may be too late to remedy. Edith Evans remains the only actor to have made me laugh at Ben Jonson without resorting to mugging or farting. Jonson, the Restoration playwrights and Shakespeare are hard, quite possibly too hard now – it may be time to move on. Perhaps that is what the young actors are telling us.

But I think there is something more structural that makes acting so unattended, and it comes in part out of government strategy with regard to the arts. How can government policy impact on the condition of speaking? I think it can, and of course it does. There is a fall-out from government thinking on the arts which encourages the ignoring of essentials, assuming them to be givens, or in some way beside the point, in a world defined by the efficacy of initiatives. Subsidies since 1979 have come with prescriptions that amount to censorship, prescriptions of two kinds, both coming out of an almost sadistic attack on the old liberal consensus. The first is managerial, the second is social. Successive administrations since then have wished upon the theatre, a traditionally well-managed trade, the problems they have perceived of management elsewhere. But how did theatre last so long as a purely commercial enterprise under political censorship without sound management? Where was marketing invented if not in the theatre? So, costly new management structures and ways of thinking about administration, born out of ignorance and ideological bias, are forced upon the theatre. And since recent government's social policy is made out of an unforgiving economic model, it seeks to shift onto all its agencies, whatever, wherever they are, concerns that are not theirs. There is a centralised determination, not only of how things are to be run and managed but of what they are, and what they are for, all out of thinking derived from the needs of the market, which in the case of the arts ignores the considerable work done in the past about what art is and what its social dimensions are, resulting in untutored depositions of how they should be. A reminder of the Dome fiasco is always overdue.

In respect of theatres, the government is like a bad actor, generalising and working on the periphery, without attending to the main intention. There is no recognition of what it is about the theatre that makes it so worthy of access and what could be done to improve it. And there is a paradox here, too, for policies derived from the current economic model make ideas of access an unobtainable fantasy. There is a ludicrous element to the present obsession with things peripheral. There is, for example, a government agency which seeks to provide artists with something called 'dream time'. This is not a fancy dreamed up by Evelyn Waugh; there is a committee funded to talk about such things and to award cash. Most artistic directors, whatever their natural bent, are being increasingly turned into government apparatchiks as they struggle to reach targets entirely beside the main purpose. A certain kind of plausible but not very able face is becoming preferred. Any faith in the idea that the Arts Council is at arm's reach from the government has long since gone. Restriction by government, ferried through the Arts Council, is greater than it has ever been. Most of the progressive ideas about inclusion in theatre come from men and women at the grass roots; subsequent bolt-on solutions dictated from on high are inauthentic. The theatre has now become over-professionalised and over-managed.

How does all this impact on acting and speaking? By implication it must. Anything as germane as speaking is beyond the understanding of arts administration as it stands. How could you sell it to the bureaucrats as internationalist?

But the problems are not only external. One of the interconnecting strands of directing which emerged in the last century has prevailed over the other. There has been a development coming out of the work of Craig which when it is at its most divergent is at its most exciting. I think of Tadeusz Kantor or the Bread and Puppet Theatre or the performance art of the American painters, of Joseph Beuys and others, where there is no text to speak of and acting is notional, yet something is produced from the dramatic idea that is vital and new. In Britain now there is a bastard version of this prevailing – a kind of training college experimentalism which relies on poor and whimsical texts and for the most part indifferent performers, and though it has an air of well-meaning progressiveness, the subtext is a kind of worried, middle-brow disregard for singular creativity, which finds talent undemocratic and unmanageable. Even more apparently old-school directors are convinced of their authorial destiny. Here is no place for acting of the kind I have been talking about, where serious theatre is being squeezed between show business and student drama, between commercial theatre and art theatre. There has been, too, an entirely misdirected reaction to the dependence on marquee names with no improvement of product. Dismantling the star system had a sensible object: to prevent stars from playing the wrong parts, not to have directorial stooges in the wrong parts instead. The business of what acting can be, and responsibility for or interest in speaking, is outside this remit.

In the opera house, the separation of the music and the drama into two different texts is now the norm. The directorial interpretation and the sound world, no matter how complementary, are no longer the one an expression of the other, if they ever were. In the theatre there is growing a similar approach to classical productions without an understanding that the text can't really be separated out in the same way as music from drama in the opera house. It may be that, since the days when prose first won out over verse, the idea of a certain kind of theatre has always been thought defunct, and the classics are now seen as vehicles for interpretation, but without the necessary technical equipment, that takes them beyond demonstration. What is needed is something radically different. Classical productions, at present, like many of the other arts are caught up in pseudo-progressive and insular conventions and in a notional transgression are being simply caught up in modish trappings.

It may be that the criticism of the young actors that I have been talking about is a blind, that there never was, except in exceptional circumstances, very good speaking, merely a conventional class-based elocution; that from the time of Shakespeare there has been a move away from the purely rhetorical which has brought us to where we find ourselves now; and that the speaking we now criticise simply reflects this and offers a challenge either to reform, radically change, or sink into irrelevance.

Rodney Ackland [1908–91], actor and playwright (*Absolute Hell*)

Bronson Albery [1891–1971], theatre director and impresario

William Archer [1856–1924], critic and journalist

Antonin Artaud [1896–1948], French playwright, poet, actor and director. His book *The Theatre and its Double* was the manifesto of the Theatre of Cruelty

Harley Granville Barker [1877–1946], actor, director, dramatist and author

Lilian Baylis [1874–1937], manager of the Old Vic and founder of Sadler's Wells

Hugh 'Binkie' Beaumont [1908–73], theatre manager and head of producers H M Tennent

Max Beerbohm [1872–1956], writer and critic

Michael Benthall [1919–74], director; Director of the Old Vic 1953–61

Joseph Beuys [1921–86], German artist

James Bridie [1888–1951], playwright, screenwriter and surgeon

Dion de Boucicault [1793–1859], writer

Edward Bulwer-Lytton [1803–73], writer

Lewis Casson [1875–1969], actor

Nikolai Cherkasov [1903–66], Russian actor who played Ivan the Terrible in Eisenstein's films

William Congreve [1670–1729], Restoration playwright

Noël Coward [1899–1973], actor, playwright, composer

Edward Gordon Craig [1872–1966], actor, director, designer and artist; son of Ellen Terry

Sergei Eisenstein [1898–1948], Soviet film director and theorist

Edith Evans [1878–1976], actress

Theodor Fontane [1819–98], German novelist and poet

John Galsworthy [1867–1933], novelist and playwright

William Gaskill, director

J T Grein [1862–1935], Dutch-born theatre impresario and drama critic

Robert Helpmann [1909–86], Australian dancer, actor, director and choreographer

Seymour Hicks [1871–1949], actor-manager, playwright and early film star

Annie Horniman [1860–1937], pioneer of the modern repertory theatre movement

Henrik Ibsen [1828–1906], Norwegian playwright

Henry Irving [1838–1905], actor-manager

Barry Jackson [1879–1961], founder of Birmingham Repertory Theatre

Tadeusz Kantor [1915–90], Polish theatre director and designer

Theodor Komisarjevsky [1882–1954], Russian theatre director and designer

Somerset Maugham [1874–1965], English playwright, novelist and short-story writer

Gerald du Maurier [1873–1934], actor-manager

Vsevolod Meyerhold [1874–1940], Russian director

Laurence Olivier [1907–89], actor, director and first Director of the National Theatre

John Osborne [1929–94], playwright

Anthony Page, director

Arthur Wing Pinero [1855–1934], writer

Nigel Playfair [1874–1934], actor-manager of the Lyric Theatre, Hammersmith in the 1920s

William Poel [1852–1934], actor and theatrical manager, founder of the Elizabethan Stage Society

J B Priestley [1894–1984], writer and broadcaster

Terence Rattigan [1911–77], dramatist

Thomas Robertson [1829–71], dramatist and actor

Elizabeth Robins [1862–1952], American born actress (first English production of *Hedda Gabler*) and writer (*Votes for Women*)

Michel St Denis [1897–1971], French actor, director and theorist whose ideas on actor training had a profound influence

Richard Brinsley Sheridan [1751–1816], writer

Githa Sowerby [1876–1970], writer (*Rutherford and Son*)

Konstantin Stanislavsky [1863–1938], Russian director and founder of the Moscow Art Theatre

Alfred Sutro [1863–1933], writer

Sybil Thorndike [1882–1976], actress

J E Vedrenne [1867–1930], manager with Granville Barker of the Court Theatre

Richard Wagner [1813–83], German composer, conductor and essayist

Oscar Wilde [1854–1900], writer

Harry Andrews as Bolingbroke in Shakespeare's *Henry IV* at Stratford, 1951
(Mander & Mitchenson Theatre Collection)

HARRY ANDREWS

*Were you influenced by a particular teacher, director or colleague at
an early stage in your career?*

There was a marvellous voice teacher at Stratford in those days, called Iris
Warren. I think she has a pupil who works there now. She was enormously
helpful – not on how to speak Shakespeare or anything like that, but how
to breathe, how to use one's voice. I used to use too much voice and get a
nodule, and she helped me to bypass that.

I never went to drama school, I went straight into repertory at the
age of 20. I tried to be an artist for a bit, and I was going to be a priest;
I also had the idea of becoming a professional cricketer for Kent. Then
a policeman. Fortunately, I met up with somebody in Wales, a lady who
had influence in the theatre. She said 'You don't want to be a policeman,
do you? What do you really want to do?' I said, 'I want to be an actor.'
My father was a doctor and a very good amateur actor, and he took us to
the theatre every fortnight to Tunbridge Wells Opera House, where they
had pre-London and après London shows. One saw all the great actors in
classical work, so I developed a taste for it. I wrote to Barry Jackson at
Birmingham Rep and got a polite reply, wrote to H M Tennent and got a
polite reply, and that was as far as I could get. But then I did get a job at
Liverpool Rep as ASM, playing understudies and little parts.

Who was directing?

Billy Armstrong. Sir William Armstrong, as he became. I had two seasons
there, and I began to get better parts. Then Gladys Cooper and Raymond
Massey came up to see a show in which I was playing a rather effective
little part, and I was offered a role in their next production at the St
James's Theatre – *Worse Things Happen at Sea*. The notices said, 'Worse
things happen at sea? I don't believe it…' But one or two people happened

to come and see it and I got quite good notices in the small part of John the footman, playing croquet on the drawing room carpet. John Gielgud [1904–2000] saw it and I was asked to go and play Tybalt in his production of *Romeo and Juliet* at the New Theatre, with Larry [Olivier: 1907–89] and Gielgud alternating Romeo and Mercutio, and Peggy Ashcroft [1907–91] as Juliet. That was really my introduction into the classical theatre, though I'd played things like the Bloody Sergeant in *Macbeth* at Liverpool.

When I was a child, I met Tyrone Guthrie [1900–71], because his father was a great friend of my father. They played bridge together. I remember meeting this enormous six foot seven creature, wound round with a great scarf, straight down from Oxford or Cambridge, saying, 'Hello, little boy, who are you?' I was so impressed by him. And of course later on in life one met him and got to know him and his wife well. He's my favourite director, I think. Naughty of course.

Was it at the Old Vic that you worked with him?

The first production I was ever involved with Tony on was *School for Scandal* in John Gielgud's 1937 season at the Queen's. Then I was Wolsey in *Henry VIII* at Stratford in 49. I was lean, so I had to be padded out and double-chinned and everything, but it was a wonderful part to play. But naughty Tony Guthrie wanted things a bit different. 'They all know that great farewell speech, they'll all be following it. Don't make a meal of it, you know, just throw it away.' Well, I thought, I don't see how you can throw away a speech like that, you really can't, it's such a great speech. I was six foot, and I had a little Cromwell. Down we went into the orchestra pit at the end, and there was laughter, particularly from Harold Hobson.

This was from throwing it away?

And the fact that it was slightly comical. So I took note of this and started to play it as I thought it should be played. A week later Tony Guthrie came round to my dressing room and said 'Harry, you were right. I'm sorry. Now you're doing it your way and it's the right way.'

How did you do it?

I played it for all it was worth, without going too far, I hope. It's a wonderful speech.

ACTORS SPEAKING

*There's something very important about an actor who has a strong
instinct for doing something a particular way...*

But if you're playing what for you is a much older man, you do have to
take guidance from your director.

*Exactly, but I would have thought he should have seen that it wasn't
working.*

Yes, he should have, and he realised it too late. But T C Worsley, one of
our great critics, who wrote in the *New Statesman*, came and saw it a
second time and gave the most wonderful notice. He also wrote a made-
up dialogue of the scene he imagined between us – Guthrie saying 'Harry,
I think you should throw it away' – and it was more or less true.

Which other directors were an influence?

Glen Byam Shaw [1904–86] I would put as number one, at his height. He
was so sensitive and helpful, and very strong. If he thought you could take
criticism, he gave it to you full blast. If on the other hand he thought an
actor didn't want criticism or couldn't take it, he wouldn't bother. Lovely
director.

*But he would be able to find another way of giving you the
information, would he?*

Well, I can only speak from my own experience. He knew that I was
sensitive and vulnerable, and would say, 'Harry, I think you know you're
being a little over-sentimental' or 'Find the wit of the part' or something.
Emlyn Williams [1905–87], who hadn't acted for some years, came to
play Iago to my Othello. After a fortnight's rehearsal, Glen Byam Shaw
said to him in front of the whole company, 'Emlyn, I think perhaps you're
illustrating all those wonderful speeches too much, you know, the words
speak for themselves', which was oh so right. Emlyn hadn't acted with
other people for many years; he did a lovely solo performance. He said
'Oh dear...' Long pause. Then: '...Glen, I think you should give me at
least four days to go back to the Arden Hotel and unlearn everything I've
done in front of the mirror...' He'd done it like his one-man show, you

see, rehearsed everything in front of the mirror. He spoke it beautifully of course.

Did Glen Byam Shaw have a particular attitude to the text?

I wouldn't say he had a particular attitude, other than getting the sense of the poetry. And don't chop up the verse.

Are you talking about end-stopping? Do you know what is meant by that?

I think I understand that, but one's instinct is not to do that. I use the punctuation as it is written – use a full stop when it's there, or a dash, or whatever. And you've got to lift to the end of the line a bit, to keep it going.

Lift to the end of the line?

Well, not obviously, but instinctively one does that in order to keep the suspense going. It's a mistake, for me personally, to do things too consciously. I think I have a good instinct about the classics, and I trust it. If I'm wrong, then I like to be told.

Have there been times when you've been made very conscious of your verse-speaking? Has anyone really overpowered you in terms of 'Say it like this'?

Never. I worked a lot with Michael Redgrave [1908–85], who was a great verse speaker. He insisted that he wasn't an intellectual actor; I think he was. He was an instinctive actor but he had a very good brain, and he knew all about feminine endings. So did John [Gielgud], and he, I suppose, was my first influence. I played Horatio with him. I think it rather shocked him to think that I was going to give my Horatio to his Hamlet in New York, but as they couldn't afford Jack Hawkins, they had to have me.

Why did it shock him?

He was disappointed. I was comparatively young and inexperienced.

What was he like to work with? Did you find yourself copying his style?

ACTORS SPEAKING

Well, I listened of course, like we all do. Alec Guinness and I were both playing small parts, and we listened. Then when it came to Alec playing Richard II and me playing Bolingbroke at the New Theatre in 1947, both of us remembered vividly how John had said, 'Down I come...' or any of the speeches. Alec was so terrified of copying that he went against it and wasn't really very good. But John... one shall never forget how some of those great speeches were said by John. 'How all occasions...' But the quiet ones were so wonderful; he never went over the top. Sometimes the voice did sing a little too much. And I would think, 'Ah ha ha! I'm never going to do that.'

Do you think people felt almost obliged to speak in the manner of John Gielgud?

No, I don't think so, but people did, and they walked with their knees bent and all that sort of thing.

And were other actors as influential?

Take an actor like Paul Scofield, who I admire enormously and who has given some definitive performances – he has an extraordinary way of speaking, which nobody, I think, should try and copy. He has a vast range and gives extraordinary interpretations which are nearly always totally convincing.

Did you react against Gielgud?

Not consciously, but subconsciously. I thought, well, it's amusing to hear you go over the top and sing like a lark and all that. But it's the truth of the performance that matters the most, and he's a lovely true actor. I think he thought, 'Now I'm expected to sing, because we're getting near the end of the play', and he was counting the house. His brain was so quick, he could do three things at once: count the house, say his speech and wink at the other actor on stage. The same with Larry: he could do wicked things just before going on, and even on stage – things that I couldn't tolerate, because I'm not that sort of actor. I've got to concentrate totally on what I'm going to do. I remember before going on in *Measure for Measure* we would wait in what was called the assembly area and Alan Badel [1923–82], a very volatile person and very keen to be a director, would sidle up to me and say 'You know John's doing that quite wrong. I think it's dreadful the way that scene is directed.' And eventually I had to really slap him down. I said, 'Alan, if ever you talk to me off-stage before I'm going on again, I shall kill you. So please remember that.'

To return to our questions. What do you think is meant by good speaking?

Well, first of all, I think you've got to be understood and it's got to be clear. It's got to be well spoken, very clearly understood. I think one of the most important things, when an actor is preparing, is to look at the text and think of it in various different ways: How would this character say these lines? I only speak for myself. Every actor's approach is different. Larry is an entirely different story. He approaches most parts from the outside.

Meaning that he knows what makes a good effect?

Yes. And the kind of noises to make, and where to reach a climax, and all that, which I don't go along with necessarily, although he makes great effect with them.

Which playwrights have inspired you, apart from Shakespeare of course?

Well, he is the greatest of all, no question. But Chekhov is of course a delight. And some modern playwrights I have enjoyed playing enormously. Terence Rattigan I think was very fine, and Edward Bond.

Oh good, I wanted to talk to you about that...

The imagery that he can produce, and the poetry – quite remarkable. As soon as I read that script of his *Lear*, I thought I've got to do it, however difficult it's going to be. I begged him and Bill Gaskill [director] to cut it. They wouldn't. I'd played in three productions of *King Lear*, so I had that sort of background to the play.

So did you regard Lear *by Edward Bond any differently, or did you approach it just as you would...*

Totally different. But in the back of one's mind was the memory of that great play of Shakespeare's. For Bond to have written that play was the most extraordinarily courageous thing to do. It was a tremendously emotional experience, and I think Bill Gaskill did a wonderful job on that small stage at the Royal Court. I just wish that some of the great speeches could have been cut. I thought it was too much. Not because of the cruelty of it – just cut in time.

What was the greatest experience you've had in a Shakespeare role?

There are two. Firstly, because I think it was the first time it ever happened, to go through the history cycle playing Bolingbroke, with a wonderful collection of people – Richard Burton as Hal and so on. That was a wonderful experience because it's like one great role, through to the dying king in *Henry IV Part 2*. And the other one, of course, is Othello, because that's a great, great play and a great part, and I was fortunate enough to be directed very well in it by Glen Byam Shaw.

In such parts, how important is the flow in long speeches?

I think it's vital. You can take a breath of course, but you can't suddenly stop.

Breaking up lines seems to be quite a popular habit.

I don't approve of it. I don't like it. I think it ruins sense. You've got to maintain the sense of a line, and the poetry, even if it's blank verse. I use the punctuation, which is there very clearly in all the great writers, but not chop it up into pieces and take a pause in order to gain a little extra emotion. It doesn't work for me.

What do you look for when you're studying one of those great speeches?

Well first of all the meaning, and the emotion, what the scene is about, but you look for the climaxes.

Do you mean the emotional climaxes?

The vocal climaxes. Obviously one has to look for those because you've got to have light and shade, build to a climax. Then, you can't keep it sustained at the same temperature; you've got to find ways of dealing with it, it can't all be on a high. But that is an instinctive thing, and when you've got good actors to play with, who respond to what you're doing, then it all comes together. And if you've got a good director who will say, 'Well I think it would be better if you withdrew that a little bit, and leant on that a bit more.' One needs help. You can't do it all on your own.

You enjoy being directed?

By a good director, yes. I hate being directed by a bad director. I feel I can do better. But I've been extremely fortunate. I can't think that I've had a bad director in the theatre. In films, yes. Television yes.

Do you approach a classical part in the same way as a modern one,
or a comedy the same as a tragedy?

I read everything I'm sent from an entirely fresh point of view. I think, 'This is a play they've asked me to do. Do I like the play? What do I think of the part?' Then if I say 'Yes', I really delve into it. I love doing research. When I was playing Lord Allenby in *Ross*, with Alec Guinness, I loved going into everything I could about Allenby. He was a lovely poet, you know, like Wavell. At the moment, I'm steeping myself in these characters in the Sackville-West. Those things I find fascinating and well worth the trouble of going into.

You tend to hide from us any idea that you consciously think about
the way you approach a speech, actually speaking it.

If you really want to know the truth about my approach to a part or a speech, I find I trust my instinct more than anything else. I know it's good, I know what sounds good and what sounds bad, and I know what my capabilities are. Rather than work too much on how I'm going to say the speech, I feel it's all there in the text, it's easy to interpret.

But instinct is governed by our generation, by who has influenced us.
Do you think there's been a change in the way people speak now?

I have the impression there has, yes.

In what way?

Perhaps the danger for young actors is that they desperately don't want to copy the old way of speaking. They feel it's all a bit old hat and it's much

ACTORS SPEAKING

better to try and modernise it, almost to think in modern vernacular. And you can't always hear because they gabble a bit. This is an old actor speaking...

Presumably you never had to change your accent, get rid of any regional accent?

No. But I enjoy playing dialect. I can give you any kind of dialect you like. Irish, West Country, Scottish or American. I enjoy that, but it's harder work of course. I speak with a normally well educated voice, I suppose.

If an actor is speaking badly, then what is it he's doing?

Various things. He's not enunciating very well, he's either very flat, or totally lacking in a sense of verse or poetry or music. On the other hand, there's a great danger in being too aware of the music in a piece. I think you're capable, even if you aren't born with a good voice, of learning how to speak. If you really work at it and go to a good teacher. But there was Alan Badel, one of the most brilliant actors I've ever worked with, who unfortunately was tone deaf. I think it was because he was in the paratroopers during the war and was shelled. So when he played Hamlet, those great speeches, although he played them brilliantly, were colourless. And this spoilt what could have been a very, very remarkable performance.

So you have to be able to hear what your voice is doing. Being in the character from an acting point of view isn't enough?

I don't think so, no. Once you've learnt it and rehearsed it and you know what you want to do with it, then your instinct takes over. When you're feeling it, it comes out as it should, not consciously as something beautiful or dramatic. Comedy, of course, is different, because that is much more technical, in my opinion.

Do you approach comedy differently?

Well yes, and it's most enjoyable. Again, it's largely instinctive, but you know the points where you're going to get laughs, and that is a question of technique. Whereas dramatic acting isn't a matter of technique, for me anyway. Many actors would disagree with me.

Have you ever been taken by the beauty of the sound you're making?

If one starts being moved and delighted by the way you are saying a line, then you're in trouble.

So you don't consciously go for that?

I know it's a beautiful line, but I don't want to be conscious of the fact that it's moving. If I move myself too much that can be fatal, I think.

Is learning about breathing very important to you?

Very important. Particularly now when I have chronic bronchitis. In the old days I had a tremendous amount of lung power and it wasn't a great problem.

What did Iris Warren teach you?

Breathing, but also the actual production of the voice. I was using far too much strangulated voice, not releasing from the throat. She went about it in a very simple way. She used to put me on my back and do relaxing exercises, making noises, not doing speeches. Then at the end you probably did a little song, actually used your vocal chords to the full. That was jolly good.

Who suggested you go to her?

I think she came round and said, Look, you're in trouble and I think I can help. I was playing Macduff, which is a killer. Although it's not a very long part, you really have got to know how to use your voice without straining it. And so emotional... Many an actor has lost his voice playing that part.

Thank you very much indeed. That was a great afternoon.

Thank you, boys, and thank you for making your way to Sussex.

GABRIELLE DAYE

How did you begin as an actress?

Oh, I had voice production lessons from the age of twelve, at school. I am one of those actresses who was educated at a convent. We had lessons from a professor of elocution who was attached to the Manchester College of Music – the Northern College of Music as it is now. I used to go home spouting reams of poetry. It was never difficult for me to learn things by heart. When the lessons finished at school, my mother sent me privately to the Morden Grey Academy in Manchester. Mother was stagestruck herself, and I think she wanted to encourage me.

Did you go to drama school after that?

No, I've never been to a drama school, never been taught how to act at all. I went as a student to the Rusholme Rep, before this last war, about 1935 I think. We had people there like Wendy Hiller, Betty Jardine, George Hagan, Eileen Draycott. My first part was in *The Dear Departed*, where I played the granddaughter. That's a Lancashire comedy, where they're having the grandfather's funeral, and I come down the stairs and say 'Grandpa's getting up!' That was a big laugh because I did it quite unselfconsciously, and it was discovered I was good at comedy. From there I went on tour in *Love on the Dole*. We had long tours then and it was always rumoured that it was coming in to London. It was either going to be London next week or Ashton under Lyme. It was usually Ashton under Lyme.

Would you say you were influenced by any particular teacher, colleague or director at this early stage?

Gabrielle Daye, 1937
(Mander & Mitchenson Theatre Collection)

Not really, no. I used to imitate various other actresses. Betty Jardine was a great one. I thought she was lovely. She made a great hit of *The Corn Is Green*, the original production.

So did you employ the elocution lessons you had been given?

Not consciously till I joined a Shakespeare company – then I did, and it came in very useful. I could always be heard, of course. I was taught to sound my consonants and the beginnings and ends of words. When I came to London, one would go to see a show which was probably going to be sent on tour, and try to make yourself look like an actress in it. I saw Patricia Hayes in *When We Are Married*. Well, I couldn't look like Patricia Hayes in a million years, but I went on tour playing her part.

Her part?

She had made a great hit as the maid, Ruby. She was absolutely marvellous. I'm not in the least bit like her, I wish I was, but I played that part on tour with Rob Wilton as the photographer. Now that taught me a lot about timing – he was wonderful, and not a jealous comedian at all.

Who directed that?

Basil Dearden [1911–71], who was the stage manager of the first production under Basil Dean [1887–1978]. Basil Dean produced it very well indeed, but was a bit of a Tartar, I believe.

Everybody says that.

Yes, I remember I worked with Beatrice Varley who played a part in it and she said he reduced everybody to tears. She told me that he changed things so much that she just went back to doing what she had done originally and he said, 'Oh well, that's fine.'

Rob Wilton was a music hall artist, wasn't he?

Yes. But he started in what they call stock. The Stock Company in Liverpool. They used to tour two or three old plays, and they never needed to change their repertoire. There was no television, and he trained in straight theatre as far as you can.

But did he tell you how to say things? Did anybody?

Oh no. Basil Dearden did a little bit, but one just rather copied Basil Dean's production, and it was very funny.

What do you think is meant by good speaking?

First of all you have got to be audible. And if you can possibly produce a beautiful sound, that is a great help too, because I don't think people want to listen to harsh voices. You sound your consonants and you end your words.

What is an actor doing if he's speaking well?

Not chewing his words up. It takes a lot of practice, I dare say, especially if you've got to tear a passion to tatters, but if you're talking about speaking in the theatre, which I presume you are, you need a director who will go to the back of the circle and say, 'What was that you said?'

What about the changes in speaking in the theatre that have happened in your lifetime?

I think the changes have come about since the war, mostly from the changes in plays, quite honestly. When I came to London people used to say, 'Oh, you've got a North Country accent', so I took care to try to iron it out. But now they don't. If you have a dialect or an accent of some kind now, you cultivate it because a lot of the plays are written for people from different strata, and they're not just drawing room comedies.

But do you think it makes any difference, apart from the natural rhythm of the accent, to whether you are speaking well?

Well it's hard to attune yourself. I saw *Troilus and Cressida* at the RSC last week, and Thersites was played with a full Tyneside accent, and quite honestly, I barely understood it. This fellow was very good, I'm not saying he wasn't, and he seemed to score quite a hit in the part, but I couldn't really tell what he was saying.

Would you approach speaking a classical and a modern role in the same way?

Oh dear, I wondered about this question. No, I don't suppose I would – I mean how does one approach a role? You just read the script. I suppose with a classical play, even the way you enter has to have much more of a pose about it, to prepare an audience for it I think. In a modern role, well, you can just sidle on and become part of the furniture.

And approaching the speaking of the text…?

I think you don't give the modern text the value that you do to a Shakespearean or a poetic text. Breathing of course is very important, isn't it? Breath control. The method I was taught in voice production was the rib-lateral or intercostal method. You take the breath into the lower part of the ribs, you flatten the diaphragm. In singing I had an exercise where you would take in as deep a breath as you possibly can, then let it out very slowly. I could count up to thirty doing that. I don't think I can do it now. Sold my piano since then. But that's very good control.

If an actor is speaking badly, what is he doing?

Well, not articulating the words, or enunciating, slurring over the key word in the phrase, perhaps. You've got to pick out what's important.

When you began to do radio, did that alter how you spoke in the theatre?

Not really no. I always hate the sound of my own voice actually. I couldn't bear myself on radio or television. Fortunately you can't see a theatre production. I think the difference between television and the theatre is that if you are in close shot, you mustn't be mouthing, that's all I can say. You just think. The words are almost unnecessary. I don't know, I'm still learning.

Was working with Geoffrey Kendal your first experience of Shakespeare?

Yes. I joined Geoffrey and Laura Kendal's – Felicity Kendal's parents – company, and swam in at the deep end. Laura Liddell, as she was then, was a very good actress, I thought. I played all the second parts, like Maria in *Twelfth Night* and Emilia in *Othello*. Geoffrey did the production, but as we did a different play every night it was more or less thrown on, you know. I remember after the death scene at the end of *Othello*, Laura, who was dead as Desdemona, opened her eyes to watch me, she thought I was so good, which was rather a nice compliment. I also played Ariel, and Saint Joan when Laura couldn't do it as she was having a baby and couldn't wear the armour. She was very cross I remember. Laura was quite an inspiration, she was the loveliest Ophelia I've ever seen. I saw Felicity do Ophelia, and I thought, 'That's Laura', but where Laura learnt it, I don't know. She had been on tour with one of the old barnstormers... Edward something. I worked with Robert Donat [1905–58] – now, what a voice! – but that was later, during the war. I was rung up to go into *The Glass Slipper*, a beautiful Christmas show he put on, and I thought it was a friend of mine pulling my leg. 'Just a moment' the secretary said, and then Robert came on to the line – well, there's no mistaking that voice – I nearly dropped the phone.

How long were you with the Kendals?

About a year, I think. We kept writing home for money. We did a different play every night and two matinees, and they did work for schools as well.

How did you rehearse?

You rehearsed during the day, just mornings, I think. They were more or less fit-ups, you know, there weren't great slashings of scenery or lights. We had costumes, and you just had to learn the lines. I remember being thrown on for Anne Page in *The Merry Wives of Windsor* which I hadn't learnt at all. I don't quite know what I said at the end, when we go round being fairies – I think I said the alphabet three or four times. I remember passing out afterwards with shock. That was really quite frightening.

Do you apply different rules to prose and verse in Shakespeare?

Well, with iambic pentameter, you do more or less keep those beats. Everybody does it differently, but we were the old school where you had to give the full vocal powers to it. Now you play it more conversationally. I don't think John Gielgud did though. I remember his Hamlet – terrific speed he went at, and it was absolutely wonderful. But then you know he's one in a million. Yes, you have to be aware of the musicality of it, and be aware of the beat as well.

Do you find it easier to work using your natural accent?

No… It is easy of course because I can recollect it, but sometimes I find I haven't got enough of an accent. People nowadays are much broader. But it depends entirely on the part.

How would you reconcile the classical demands of the text with the actor's personal need for expressiveness?

You have to really suit yourself to the classical demands of the text, try to convey what the author meant. You may have other feelings yourself, but I would really try to observe the text. If I fail, I fail.

So you're less worried about putting your own personality across…

Oh no. That has never really worried me. If it's a good script, you follow what the author's intentions are. You might get moulded a bit by the director, though there are remarkably few good directors.

Has the style of directing changed over your life in the theatre? How did you find working with Lindsay Anderson [director, 1923–94], for example? He's very clever with actors, I thought.

I suppose he must be. I'm a bit dim, but he didn't really try to produce me in any way, he just let me go on doing it. I personally thought he was better with actors than actresses. Peter [Gill] on the other hand is a very stimulating director, and taught me the value of just sitting still on the stage, although I've seen Sybil Thorndike do that most effectively in a play. She just sat there darning socks, and all your attention was concentrated on her. In *The Daughter in Law* Peter made me sit still and oh goodness me it was agony. Sit still without fidgeting or moving at all, and listen to this long four-and-a-half-page speech of Anne Dyson's. I felt like the snake and the rabbit, but it was very effective. You feel when you're on the stage that you've got to be doing something, whereas no, it was much more effective to be sitting there just thinking, or doing absolutely nothing. I like directors who don't tell you how to say a thing, but who can illuminate the script for you, you know, open windows. There are a few that can do that.

Are there any modern actors you particularly like?

I used to like Alan Badel – the poor darling is dead now of course.

Why did you like him?

Well, Voice Beautiful again. He had a nice resonant voice. I like the resonance in a voice, but I do like it to be heard. I like the enunciation also, I don't like it all rolled into one. I was talking about Robert Donat earlier, and he had a beautiful voice, a wonderful resonant voice. He was very good at verse-speaking too, he used to always do the New Year's Eve broadcast on the radio, 'Ring Out Wild Bells'. I suppose you're born with it, but you can practise and achieve more resonance in the head, you know. I don't like to listen to an actor who's thinking, 'I'm going to give you this, this is my voice.' It's got to be natural, not artificial.

FABIA DRAKE

*Your biography tells us that you acted in both French and English and
that you were influenced by Georges Le Roy.*

Very much so. He was a Sociétaire from the Comédie Française and I
was fortunate enough to be taught diction by him at a perfectly ordinary
finishing school in Paris. Then I was 16, but I had started training at the
age of nine. I was the youngest student ever to attend the Royal Academy
of Dramatic Art, which was then the ADA, and at the age of nine I was
influenced by a particular teacher there called Mrs McKern. She was a
brilliant voice production teacher and she brought my voice, at the age of
nine, down three tones, which was very valuable. It wasn't a high voice, but
she thought I needed a lower tone and she worked in a most unexpected
manner.

But didn't you feel restricted by that?

No, I wanted to get this deeper voice. It didn't restrict me at all, it
enhanced. I was playing the big men's parts at nine.

*So you were obviously determined from a very young age to be an
actress.*

Yes, from the age of two, shall we say, but I don't think that's relevant
to our conversation. What we're talking about is the fact that I was able
to start so early, and this business of consonants. When I came to work
with Georges Le Roy on French diction, he taught me to use my lips,
which you don't in English, and this has helped me. I came back from
France speaking better English, although I never spoke a word of English
the whole time I was there.

When you were teaching at RADA, were there any technique classes?

There was always diction and elocution and voice production, but no classes for stage technique, which is a different thing. One discovers what one doesn't know when you come to teach other people.

Which colleagues do you admire or have you been influenced by?

I was enormously influenced by a wonderful lady called Marie Tempest [1864–1942], with whom I was lucky enough to work when I was in my teens. She had one of the most perfect dictions that I have ever encountered, and because she took an interest in me I was with her in two plays, and in one of them the part of her daughter was written for me to play. She spent hours in the wings telling me how to say the words 'milk' and 'devil' because I was saying 'miuk' and 'devuw'. She paid colossal attention to speech and that was very fortunate.

Was her point of view aesthetic rather than about clarity?

Oh no, clarity is part of it, but it's aesthetic as well. One of your questions is about what speaking badly means. It means being slovenly.

Were there any of your colleagues or contemporaries you reacted against? I mean were there people you thought 'Oh God, that's awful, I'm not going to do anything like that'?

Oh no, the standard was too high. The standard of speaking in the English theatre when I was in my teens was way beyond what it is now. It was admirable.

What do you think is meant by good speaking? If an actor is speaking well, what is he doing?

Sounding his consonants. It's a neglected talent, it really is.

Someone said that the vowel sounds carry the emotion and the consonants carry the idea...

No, that couldn't be less sensible. It makes no sense at all. The consonants carry the clarity. The vowels, according to Marie Tempest, carry the truth of the word, but nothing to do with emotion. I don't know where you got that from.

Fabia Drake as Princess of the Western Regions in *Lady Precious Stream*, with Roger Livesey, Little Theatre, 1934 (Mander & Mitchenson Theatre Collection)

It's just a saying I've heard. Who among your younger contemporaries do you think speaks well?

Maggie Smith. No question. I think because she's been brought up in the classical school. I think you need classical training to speak well, because you can't be in classics without good speech.

Would you think that someone who had a regional accent could speak the classics well?

Now this is an interesting point. When I was on the staff at RADA, as a wartime job, there came into my classes various students with strong regional accents. These accents are extremely valuable and must never be obliterated. But I remember one student who had a very, very strong Scottish accent, so strong was it that you couldn't understand a word he said. I said to him 'You're completely unintelligible, and until you can speak standard English, you're not employable.' His name was Fulton Mackay [1922–87].

Ah yes. He emerged.

He did, but he didn't lose the power of the regional accent. You must never lose it, it's too valuable. But he did bring into his life a proper, acceptable, normal accent. He has a little bit of an accent but he could play without it if he wanted to.

Are there others of your younger contemporaries whom you think speak well?

Richard Pasco speaks well. I've worked with him. But I haven't got a long list of them.

Has there been a change in speaking in the theatre in your lifetime?

Yes, it has deteriorated, unquestionably. If you ask me what do I think are the influences that have helped to effect such a change – microphones. If you haven't got to learn projection, you haven't got to learn clarity. It's clarity we're back to, consonants, there aren't any.

That's interesting. Something else which has happened more recently is the advent of studio theatres, the small space...

No projection.

No, it's not required at all. The curious thing is one can go to watch plays in theatres as small as that and still not really hear what people say.

Because they've never learnt to articulate. The primary job of the actor is to be audible.

So the main influence has been the advent of the microphone.

I think so.

Both in film, television and radio, but also in the theatre?

Yes, even in a straight play they have microphones sometimes.

Yes, I have to agree with you, I'm really against that because it denies one of the most vital areas of the actor's art.

His connection with the audience.

If an actor is speaking badly, what is he doing?

Being slovenly, and probably dropping his voice at the end of lines. You need great breath control, but we'll come to that a bit later.

Talking about Shakespeare, do you apply different rules to prose and verse?

Of course not. They're all speaking.

Then there are all these questions about the rules of verse. Are you familiar with them?

I'm not interested in them at all. When we come to the last question, which is how do you handle the beat of the iambic line: You listen for the rhythm, which is inescapable. It is inescapable, the rhythm in the blank verse of Shakespeare. You can't make a mistake once you are aware of the rhythm.

And if an actor doesn't have a good sense of rhythm?

Well he's got to acquire it if he's going to play in Shakespeare. I had the enormous good fortune of playing Shakespeare from the age of nine, and playing big parts with long speeches, so I presume I learnt my job as a Shakespearean actress at that time, but I'd never had any difficulty in keeping the rhythm. I'm not interested in any of these other things – end-stopping, feminine endings, rhyming couplets and broken lines. If I was concerned with them, I'll tell you what they would do. They would interfere with what Hazlitt called in Edmund Kean his 'animating soul'. If I began to be self-conscious about that kind of thing, which has nothing to do with the purpose of playing, it would interfere with my animating soul. Are you in agreement?

Absolutely, yup.

It's a rhythm that you go for, and the sense is a different matter altogether. You phrase for rhythm because you can't escape it, you can't avoid it, but the sense is a different thing. That is the thoughts of the character that you're playing, which is the purpose in playing. You must not be distracted. The kind of concentration that is being aimed at – and surely concentration is the lynchpin of acting – must never be punctured by anything. Your concentration has to be absolute.

In the preparation of a part, how would you find the rhythm?

Well, let's go back to the part that I perhaps had the greatest success in when I was a Shakespearean actress – Rosalind. Rosalind is almost all prose, but you've only got to find the thoughts that animate the prose to find the character; and when you come to verse, all you're concerned with is that you don't despoil it by losing rhythm. But the purpose is the same: you are identifying with the thoughts of that character for every second that you're on stage.

So the real preparation of the part is in finding and understanding the thoughts of the character rather than concerning yourself with the rhythms.

Absolutely. The rhythms are incidental but essential. There's another point. You should never have to learn a part. If you read it enough it will become part of you, and that is the way to approach every part.

Read it aloud?

That is advisable. When I was working on Rosalind, I read it always aloud. It's a very long part – a third of the whole play, but I never had to learn it. I read it and read it because I wanted to absorb her.

Do you ever write out your parts?

Oh always. So does John Gielgud. We both do exactly the same. I write out every part; I don't copy it. I write it from my memory and then I go back, and if I've made a mistake, I write it again. I don't copy it because that doesn't put it in your brain. That is the way you make it flawless. You carry the lines in your head and write them out, and if you've made a mistake, you do it again. You've got to know what you're doing; you can't leave it to chance, and I'm afraid sometimes it is left to chance. It can vary, and some of the best things you ever do come unexpectedly, during performance, because by that time you and the part are one and it's expanding all the time.

Do you feel the possibilities of expansion are infinite?

Limitless. And the joy of playing great classical parts is that you never get to the end of them.

Are there any disciplines in the speaking of prose and verse that you would like to see generally applied?

Use of consonants. And bellows capacity, which comes from the diaphragm.

What about vowels?

Well they've got to be purified. And consonants must be improved, they are the secret to audibility. Breath must be developed with a bellows capacity from the diaphragm. Laurence Olivier told me once (we were very close friends) that he could not have played Macbeth in that season at Stratford if he had not first played Mark Antony, because he learned to breathe to play Mark Antony. It's done from the diaphragm, so that when you've finished with the breath that is in your lungs, you have another area of breath which you don't have to take a breath to get to.

*The modern thing is to use your back ribs. I've been helped by Cicely
Berry at Stratford, and her great thing is to involve your back as well
as your diaphragm.*

Since you've mentioned Cicely Berry, does she work on speeches that are
part of your role?

*No, she discourages one from using speeches that one is going to play,
because you have to feel special about those things. We read a lot of
poetry, and many of the exercises are just making noises.*

That's to extend your range, that's fine. The ideal range for an actor's voice
is apparently two full octaves. Somebody told me that Katina Paxinou, the
Greek actress, had exemplified this, but I shouldn't think many people
have two octaves. You see, in fear the voice is always squeezed, so these
two octaves are a valuable adjunct. You could do what they did to me to
drop my voice, which is marvellous if you're nine, much easier to do than
if you're 19. I used to work on scales with Mrs McKern on the piano:
speak 20 times on that note, and then 20 times on the one under it. And
when we got that right, we moved to the next note. But it took a lot of
work. I know that Vivien Leigh [1913–67], who was a friend of mine,
dropped her voice when she was going to play Antigone.

*How do you reconcile the actor's personal need for expressiveness
with the classical demands of the text?*

May I ask where this question comes from? It's such a strange question
because the actor has no personal need for expressiveness. The actor has a
job of creating a character. I find this a very unexpected question.

*Well, it may be that some people seem to have a need for personal
expressiveness which overrides all other considerations.*

Then they shouldn't be pretending to be actors. They should get into a
pulpit or something. It's not the business of the actor to be concerned
with his own personal need for expressiveness. It's nothing to do with
the purpose of playing. You act from an awareness that there is a world
elsewhere and a great many different kinds of characters that you
identify with, but it's got nothing to do with your own personal need for

expressiveness. It's the dramatist's intention which you have to show to an audience. If you don't show that to an audience, you're not doing your job. Tyrone Guthrie went to the try-out of *Arms and the Man* and went round to see Olivier who was playing Sergius. He said 'You despise Sergius, don't you?' And Larry said 'Yes, my God, I do!' and Tony said, 'Then you'll never be able to show him to an audience until you can sympathetically understand him.' Marvellous.

Yes, one should never make moral judgements on the characters one plays.

No, you can't. That's why actors are immensely sympathetic human beings – because they can't condemn anybody.

Gwen Ffrangcon-Davies in *The Immortal Hour*, Regent Theatre, 1922
(Mander & Mitchenson Theatre Collection)

GWEN FFRANGCON-DAVIES

*Were you influenced by a particular teacher, director or colleague at
an early stage in your career?*

I found it difficult to get into the theatre because I had no entrée. I never
went to a drama school or anything like that. The Academy had only just
started and I didn't think much of that. I did have some training with a
very kind lady who took me on and taught me a great many things which
I had to unlearn afterwards.

Did she teach you verse-speaking?

No, not verse. Nobody ever taught me verse-speaking. Such as it is, I've
taught myself and because of the knowledge I gained as a singer, you see,
I sang lieder. As I couldn't get into the theatre, and I was tired of being
in musical comedy chorus – that was hardly a career – I went back and
became a singer. And that's where I learnt to phrase, because in lieder
– Mahler, Brahms, Schumann, Schubert – the composer does it for you.
He phrases it and he interprets the words, so that when you come to speak
verse you learn to phrase, and above all have a very clear picture in your
mind, because in the beginning was the word, and the word means minds,
doesn't it? Without that, there isn't anything.

   I did have some teaching with an American lady, Mrs Manning-Hicks.
She'd had a school of acting in California, then she married and came over
here. She was a most exceptional woman. I was only about 14, I was still
at school. She was the very first person that I ever heard of who gave
readings of plays. I can see her now, very fragile little delicate American
lady with a soft American voice, in my mother's back drawing-room, with
the intelligentsia of St John's Wood to listen to her. I remember her doing
Oedipus, or a Gilbert Murray *Hippolitus*. She did Shaw's *Candida*, and
made you see the whole thing. She taught me, and she grounded me in all

the big Shakespearean female parts. So from the age of 14, I walked with Ophelia, up and down and back and forth to school, and Juliet of course lived with me from then, all through my difficult and heart-breaking years. I had ten years in the wilderness, you know, in musical comedy chorus. Not good. Not good. But, on the other hand, disciplined. Then I got my wonderful chance at the Glastonbury Festival. Then I went into music, and from music I got *The Immortal Hour*. And that's how I graduated into the theatre, through Glastonbury and *The Immortal Hour*. Then Barry Jackson said would I stay on as juvenile leading lady at the Birmingham Repertory Company, and the heavens opened after ten years of being in the wilderness.

Was that when you met Thomas Hardy?

No, I met Thomas Hardy when I was offered Tess [*of the d'Urbervilles*] in about 1925, 26.

Which other colleagues would you say you have been influenced by?

I don't think I've been influenced... Oh yes, my Ellen! [Ellen Terry, 1847–1928] When I was a child, my godmother, Miss Harris, was Ellen Terry's companion for many years, and as a little girl of five I was taken to play with a collection of dolls that Miss Terry had. She gave me, and I've got it now, a little doll's tea-set that is going to go to the Theatre Museum when I die. She was my idol. I didn't know what acting was but I knew she was a wonderful person. From the age of about six – I suppose it must have been hearing them talk about Miss Terry – I said when I grow up I'm going to be an actress. I can remember saying it very firmly and sticking to it. Then my mother met this Mrs Manning-Hicks and she took me on and she found that I was pliable. I said, 'Can I leave school because I'm not doing any good, I hate it.' My mother said, 'You can't go on the stage so young, you have to go to do Home Life Training.' I went to Sesame House Home Life Training for two years, in which I learnt how to cook, how to sew, how to sweep, how to clean the house, kindergarten training, God help me.

I took my certificate, and then Mother said, 'Now we'd better find out whether or not you've got any talents to go into the theatre.' She wrote to Miss Terry and asked if she would vet me, as it were. Very greatly daring, I went along with my mother to Miss Terry, who was in those days living in that lovely house in King's Road, Chelsea, that afterwards Peter Ustinov had. I remember it well. We stopped off to buy a sheaf of lilies to give Miss Terry, to put her in a good mood, and she was angelic. What do you suppose I did? Oh yes, just launched into the potion scene from *Romeo and Juliet*! That's what you do at seventeen. However, she said yes, yes she thought there was something there, but don't go to a school, get into the theatre. Well that was easier said than done, because at that time there was no theatre in the provinces at all. And there were no repertories. I think Miss Horniman had just started in Manchester, but that's all. The thing that I remember that Ellen Terry said to me about the potion scene, the one thing that stuck in my mind, she said she wouldn't weep during it. Evidently I'd let myself go. What she could sense, I suppose, was that I did have something that I could project and lose myself in. She said, 'There are three great I's to remember. Industry, Intelligence and Imagination, and the greatest of these is Imagination.' Now that, I've always remembered, and I think that's a pretty good directive, don't you?

Yes, very good.

So that's the way I developed through music into speech, because after all speech is really so musical, and singing is only, my father used to say, sustained speech. The thing I've always tried to find was the essential reality of whatever one is speaking, whether it's prose or poetry, and making it clear without stressing too much. I remember Tony Guthrie saying, 'Don't hit every word, take it in a sweep, making up your mind which will be the high spot. Make for that and then let the rest go.' That was when I was battling with one of those long speeches of Queen Katherine's in *Henry VIII*. I think it very sound. It certainly helped me.

What do you think an actor is doing when he is speaking well?

He's interpreting to the best of his ability what the creator has given him, to find out what the author has wanted to say, and if it's obscure, trying to find out why. Now this is an interesting thing that Ellen Terry's daughter told me, which I've just remembered: that when she was studying a Shakespeare play, she had an exercise book, with the text on one page, and opposite she transcribed it into colloquial modern English.

As a child, I heard Ellen Terry do the wooing scene with Beatrice and Benedict. In those days she did little tours in which she did an excerpt from *Much Ado*, and the death scene from Queen Katharine's death scene from Henry VIII, and *Nancy Oldfield*, which is a fraught little piece about an actress and a young man who falls in love with her. I remember seeing her do those three things when I was a child, then when I was about 18, I saw her play the Nurse in *Romeo and Juliet*, with disastrous performances by Doris Keane and Basil Sydney, I think it was, as Romeo and Juliet. Of course all the notices were taken away by the Nurse and Mercutio, who was Leon Quatermaine, and Romeo and Juliet died the death in about a fortnight. I knew the part of the Nurse because I had worked on Juliet with Mrs Manning-Hicks, and I remember thinking Ellen Terry wasn't speaking the text, going home and checking up, and finding she was. It was as if it had been written yesterday, and that's the secret, to make it absolutely contemporary, but keep its size and its colour and its stature. You mustn't speak poetry as if it was prose, because poetry is something else, but rhythm is terribly important. This is only to say the way I work... I did find when I did *The Family Reunion* with Paul Scofield and Peter Brook directed, Peter helped me a great deal. I suppose I was inclined to make it too flowery, and he made me get back to the essentials always. Another thing a lot of younger people don't realise is the tremendous importance of a pause.

Is there a different approach for prose and verse in Shakespeare?

Oh yes. The approach for prose is to make it sound as if it had been written yesterday.

And what is your approach if it's verse?

In the beginning was the word – that is really my father's gospel. You must see it in your mind's eye before you can project it to make anybody else see.

Do you think that there's a different way of approaching classical and modern work?

Well I'm not very au fait with modern poetry, but I would imagine the same rules would apply. As you know, I am 95 years old, and I am naturally of my age. I don't really care for modern music or modern poetry.

ACTORS SPEAKING

Do you admire any actors of your younger contemporaries?

Oh, I admire them enormously. I see them mostly on the box, but I find them extremely talented. My difficulty in the theatre is I don't hear so well, and that's an awful bore.

Also, perhaps modern actors don't speak so well?

Well, no, and another thing is that the poor wretches have to speak on an open stage with nothing to throw the voice back. Oh dear, that Olivier Theatre, that's my bête noire. I went to hear the *Coriolanus* and most of the words went right over my head, and I was in the front row. It was all very excitingly done and they rushed up and down and so forth. What on earth Volumnia was doing, sitting down playing cat's cradle on the stage in a very expensive white dress and a gold collar, I don't know. I said to Irene [Worth], 'Well, what was that all about?' No, not for me. I like a certain amount of common sense.

Do you admire anyone in particular of the younger generation?

Oh yes of course. The boy who's been in America for so long and has just come back to the National and he's going to do Lear – Anthony Hopkins. And then of course the other terribly good boy is the brilliant one who was so wonderful in *I Claudius* – Derek Jacobi. And I just made friends with Nigel Hawthorne who has come to live only 25 miles away. He is a very good actor.

Do you think there has been a change in speaking during your time in the theatre?

Oh yes. When I was very young I went a great deal to the theatre, always in the pit because we never had any money. I saw all of them, and they were – well, Hamlet's advice to the players about not mouthing the words…

They used to, you mean?

Oh yes, declaiming, and it drove people out of the theatre. That's why Shakespeare's plays went into a deep decline after Irving and Kean. There were great spectaculars, and people went to see scenery, but I was very young and I used to think to myself, 'Grr, don't believe a word of it!' And that's the only criterion that I've ever gone by. Is it real? Is it true? Do I believe it? I think that the young people have it in their minds very, very clearly, but they haven't always the expertise to know how to put it over. That only comes with years of practice. My Juliet was greatly praised because I was the first of the young Juliets. I wasn't all that young, but I did look excessively so, and everybody thought I was about seventeen. I was able to speak Juliet's lovely speeches, keeping the rhythm and yet making them sound as if they were just contemporary speech.

We have all these questions about verse-speaking technique – does end-stopping matter?

I don't know what it is. I don't know any of the technical things. I never was taught you see. It all came out of 'In the beginning' and Imagination. You find your own way, and you don't find it all at once, you know, but there's a great danger in having too much technique.

What about the importance of vowels and consonants and breath and variations of tone?

Oh yes, pure vowels, please. Don't let's have any of these hyphenate-diphthong things. But then you see that's how I was trained as a singer. With my father, everything started from the word. They make such a lot of fuss over this, and half the time they never really achieve that complete relaxation and freedom from down there – I was taught as a child to breathe in my diaphragm, not up here. That gives you a cushion for your voice to sit on and you won't suffer from a strained voice if your voice is cushioned and balanced on the breath. After all, breath is life, isn't it?

What about variation in tone, is that important in speaking?

Very, very, but it must come from the thought, not from 'Oh I'll make this dark or I'll make that light'. I was just thinking about the last lines of *Antony and Cleopatra*, when Antony dies, and she says, 'There is nothing left remarkable beneath the visiting moon.' Or Rosalind, she's so in love that it's nearly killing her and then she has to pretend not to be. That love scene where she says 'Oh coz, coz, my pretty little coz. Oh, that thou didst know how many fathoms deep I am in love. It cannot be sounded, it is like the Bay of Portugal.' It's those lovely changes, isn't it, sunshine and showers. And Shakespeare knew it all so perfectly, which is why he's the one. I've done so little of him. I did take over Beatrice one year at Stratford and that I adored. I have done Juliet when I was young, and Titania of course, and she's fun too. But Basil Dean was very difficult and very tiresome, not a good director. He would say, 'Don't think, dear. I'll think for you.' And I used to go home and cry with rage, so that it was not a very happy experience. But there's a lovely speech when she and Oberon are having their first quarrel scene – 'Then I must be thy lady, but I know When thou hast stolen away...' Just any wife to any husband – 'I know where you were the night before, and that girl you were with.' Paraphrase it; that's what Ellen did always, you see.

And is audibility very important?

Oh yes, terribly important, and a technical thing for audibility is consonants. Vowels will take care of themselves.

There's another question about the beauty of sound.

Yes, well, but that beauty must come from beauty of soul. In the old days when I was a child there were lots of people like Henry Irving, with a beautiful sound but nothing in the upper storey at all. It is a danger, you see. You have a beautiful voice we can all swoon away into, God gives you a beautiful voice, you are supposed to use it. But with brain.

How do you reconcile the actor's personal need for expressiveness with the classical demands of the text?

In other words how do you manage to make it convincing when Lady Macbeth talks about the daggers when she's obviously never murdered anybody? Isn't that where imagination comes in?

Yes, or how do you make it sound as if you've just thought of it and at the same time allow it to be verse?

I can't explain it, but you do keep rhythm, you do keep proportion, and that's where pauses come in. Always you're thinking of the picture that you're seeing. Unless you have that imagination, you'll never be a good actor.

Who in your experience could be imitated without being a bad influence?

Oh no, not imitated dear child. Not ever imitated. Influenced, influenced. The older ones who have something to give can influence the younger ones. But I think we really ought not think, 'Where am I going to get it from?' When I was young and first saw *Hamlet*, I went about in a daze for three days afterwards and burst into tears if anybody spoke to me.

Who played it?

It wasn't a very good performance – H B Irving [1870–1919] – I think it was the play actually. And I was sufficiently aware to think that Lily Brayton [1876–1953] as Ophelia was no good at all.

You played Ophelia to John Gielgud's Hamlet, didn't you?

No, Jessica Tandy did. No, I played Juliet to John Gielgud's Romeo. I was definitely madly influenced by Ellen Terry. And Granville Barker was my first idol (not as an actor because I never saw him act). I was once produced by him in, of all things, a musical play. What he was doing producing a musical play I shall never know. And of course it was a failure. It was way ahead of its time. Granville Barker as a director – well, he could make a cat do anything. He was really extraordinary. I can remember him saying to us, 'Ladies and gentlemen, come here please', and we were all wide-eyed because we had known about him and some of us had seen his work. 'I want you all to bring a little notebook and a pencil with you, because each of you will be an individual. You're not just a block of people doing the same thing, you are each individuals. I shall give you something to say, and you needn't necessarily say it aloud, because the heroine will probably be singing, but...' In other words, he choreographed and choreographed, and of course we were so full of enthusiasm, I've never forgotten it. I was a little fishergirl. It was set in the harbour of a Portuguese fishing village, and we were waiting for the boats to come in. I and two other girls were playing marbles or something down at the front, and Barker said, 'When you hear the call from the sea you jump up and run on the wall and wave.' I leapt up full of enthusiasm, and he said, 'Come back, little girl, come back.' So I came back, and he looked at me, and said, 'You never heard that whistle.' And of course I was so eager... Oh dear, the things one remembers.

Do you think a director is important in the theatre?

I have been very fortunate. In my early days I had H K Ayliff [1872–1949], who let me have my head and didn't interfere at all. He expected actors to be able to act, not to have to spoonfeed them. I remember we were rehearsing *The Barretts of Wimpole Street* for the Malvern Festival in 1930 or 31. I'd just finished doing the love scene and he said, 'Yes, that's it. I was wondering when you were going to start to do a bit of acting.' But he hadn't said anything. He knew I would find it. I think there's far too much of directors superimposing their ideas. Let the actor have a chance to bring things to you and see whether you like it.

When did you retire? Have you retired?

Oh yes. The last thing I did in the theatre was a small part in *Uncle Vanya* [Royal Court 1970] with Paul Scofield, and Anthony Page directing. I played the old lady, rather bluestocking girl.

So has the function of the director changed in your time?

Oh yes, tremendously, since Basil Dean and his 'Don't think, dear, I'll think for you'. I worked with a South American, Jose Quintero, on *Long Day's Journey Into Night*, and he was a wonderful director. Alan Badel and Ian Bannen played the brothers, and it was their very first beginnings, both were highly inexperienced. He worked with them on those long long speeches. It's quite absurd, really: a play with the depth of *Long Day's Journey* and you have three and a half weeks' rehearsal. It's absurd. That's why I was able to inject what I did into Juliet and the early parts I played, because of the years of study that went into them. Juliet, Ophelia, Rosalind and all the rest of them – walking up and down the streets. People must have thought I was barmy.

Had you learnt them before you played them?

Oh yes, yes, yes.

Did you work with Edith Evans? Was she a good speaker?

Oh yes, yes. She spoke beautifully. Particularly in the 18th-century plays. Oh, I can hear her Millamant, it was superlative, And she had that thing – which so often Millamants miss – that underneath that tight-boned corset there was an ardent, burning, desiring heart, just waiting. That came through all the time. It was held in check, it wasn't sort of splurged all over the place, so it was so much more provocative. And later when she did modern work – I can see her now in a play she did with Owen Nares [1888–1943]. She was the doctor and he was a clergyman, it was a St John Ervine play – *Robert's Wife*. I can see her kneeling at his feet and saying with such warmth and tenderness, 'My dear, dear husband.' Oh yes, she was a very great actress. And darling Peg [Ashcroft] has the same quality.

ALEC GUINNESS

Which voices do you hear on stage at the moment that you admire?

I'm like that kind of ghastly woman who looks round an art gallery and says, 'Well I know what I like.' I am inclined not to like what I hear going on now. The person I think speaks Shakespeare verse best that I've heard currently is Sarah Badel.

Really?

Her father was a marvellous actor...a very tiresome man but...

That's what Harry Andrews said. In fact he threatened to kill him one night.

Alan Badel threatened to kill Harry?

No, Harry threatened to kill Badel. I think it was just that Harry wanted to concentrate in the few moments before he went on stage, and Alan wanted to give everybody notes.

I only rehearsed a play with him once, in fact the original production of T S Eliot's *Cocktail Party*, and after about a week's rehearsal he suddenly screamed at all of us (there was Irene Worth, Catherine Nesbitt, Bobby Flemyng, myself and two or three others): 'None of you knows what you're fucking well doing', threw his script down and left the theatre. That was the last we saw of him. He was probably absolutely right. I mean we were only tentatively feeling our way... But he was a marvellous actor.

It's interesting, isn't it? He's part of a generation of actors that seem to have foundered on the rocks somewhere in their fifties, spent themselves early in some way. I think Badel died of a heart attack.

I don't know that he spent himself. I don't think he gave himself a chance really. He was so dismissive of so much that he was offered, and you know, you have to keep a roof over your head. I mean, lovely to be the great artist, but you've got to work with other people in this job. He was the only other actor I'm aware of who always put, as far as Shakespeare was concerned, a hair-breadth stop at the end of every line.

When I was in my early twenties, Gielgud was easily the most influential person in the theatre. He was a high romantic and everyone was besotted by him and by his voice. The place was littered with productions by him. If you look down those cast lists, he chose people whom he believed in, whether they were unheard of, like me, or not. Not like Donald Wolfit [1902–68] who cast deliberately below him, surrounded himself with inferior talent. Gielgud was exactly the opposite. I think John's way of tackling everything was based on Forbes-Robertson [1853–1937], who I suppose was the previous generation's romantic classical actor, but it was sort of modernised. I never saw Forbes-Robertson, alas, but I had an old 78 record (which went during the war) of him reading a soliloquy from *Hamlet* and some stuff from *Richard II*. It was a very poor quality recording, I suppose probably done about 1912. There was something very pleasing about it but you thought, 'Oh for God's sake get a move on', you know. Well John was the person who came and got a move on in those days. I mean it got speeded up, though it was in the same rhythm.

What was it about Laurence Olivier that was upsetting? Harry Andrews spoke of how he loved working with Olivier but made a mental note to try not to be like him.

I would have thought Harry was very much in John's vein, very disciplined.

So were they an influence on you?

Oh huge. An influence which I personally sought to banish as soon as I realised it. I didn't want to be influenced by anyone. I mean, I was very lucky in some ways working with John [Gielgud] who was very disciplinarian, but he stiffened one up so that you couldn't move with freedom. He would say, 'Make me laugh!'; 'Oh, I thought you were going to be funny!'; 'Oh you're so stiff!' And if you were playing with him, he used to say your lines under his breath (or he did with me anyway). But he

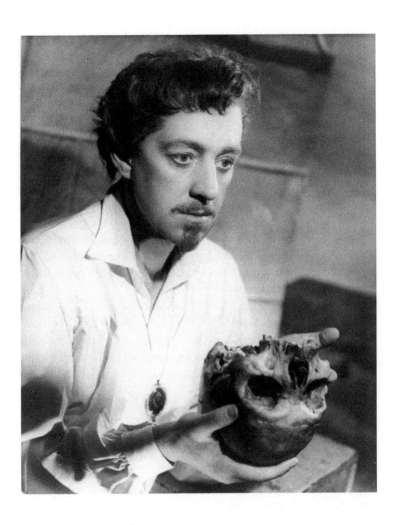

Alec Guinness as Hamlet, New Theatre, 1951
(Mander & Mitchenson Theatre Collection)

was a great actor, and had an influence in the theatre too because he was the first person to bring in new designers, directors, people like Michel St Denis [1897–1971] and so on. But it was torture and he was very, very impatient. I mean, he was dear and we all adored him but he was so impatient.

Well, going from that kind of rigid thing of John's to working with Tony [Tyrone] Guthrie, who was absolutely the opposite, was wonderful. He was wonderful with the young, and inclined to be impatient with the successful and middle-aged, and very very kind to the old who were having trouble with their waterworks. He loved diction – he had marvellous diction himself – and was a fiend for speed. You couldn't do anything fast enough for him. I mean, he wanted the sense there, but the important thing was speed. He used to want you to say five lines of Shakespeare on one breath. Although it was hugely free, one found oneself wanting to please him by being madly fast and taking huge breaths and really not troubling about anything else.

With Michel St Denis, a kind of realism came into one's life for the first time, a psychological approach to things, and a sort of French peasant-y feel for props. So I shuffled around those three, and each time, although I was happy to go to one of them, I was also happy to be rid of them because I wanted to make my own little area.

Which of the directors that you worked with at that time struck a major chord with you, do you think?

Well for me personally, I think Guthrie, because we could talk the same language and laugh at the same things. He was a great sender-upper of everything and everyone in a charming, delightful way. John, to whom I really owe my career, I respect and love dearly and know well, but I've never been totally at ease with him. Perhaps now I can sit down at a table with him and we can chat, because he really only wants to gossip anyway. But with Guthrie you could chat, gossip, be easy, say anything you wanted, reveal yourself or discuss the substance of a play or a part, all in the same way. You didn't put on your actor's hat to sit at his feet. He was always teasing one out, to get your own feelings or thoughts.

What, in your opinion, is meant by good speaking?

Well, absolutely everything has been said by Shakespeare in the speech to the Players. I don't think you can fault it. It's got to have life, hasn't it? Presumably what that means is not doing pyrotechnics, necessarily, it's keeping the light life to it, and clarity too. Maybe I'm going deaf, but I went to *The Chalk Garden* last night, the Ronald Eyre production at Chichester, and I enjoyed it very much indeed, but I was sitting in about the fifth row, and apart from two not very brilliant performers in the small parts whom I could hear absolutely, I missed yards of it, really yards. Now it's a beast of a theatre I know. I've only played there twice and maybe the nature of the play and its slightly artificial language needs a small setting to make it glitter. Spread round like that it's sort of muffled. I did enjoy my evening and found the play infinitely better than I'd remembered it.

Apparently Googie Withers had a terrible experience the other night in that play, a lady came and joined her on the stage... The play starts with three people coming to be interviewed for a job, and that's when the woman appeared, so the audience accepted it totally for a bit, until she turned round and denounced the name of theatre, saying, 'I wanted to see *Annie Get Your Gun*, not this!'

I just wanted to ask, going back to people who have influenced you,
which European directors – or is it just a matter of taking bits and
pieces from different people?

Michel St Denis was an influence, definitely. Not that I trusted him whole-heartedly, he was too pernickety, but he was something of an eye-opener to the English theatre when he arrived on these shores to direct in English for the first time, Obey's *Noah* [in which Guinness played the Wolf, 1935]. I don't think the theatre then was anything like as bad as people think it was, I mean there were some marvellous performers and indeed some jolly good plays, which didn't necessarily get heard of again because things had much shorter runs. St Denis was the first person who made one very conscious of the imagination of physical things. The best example I can give was at the start of his London Theatre Studio drama school, which eventually went to Islington but which started in Diaghilev's old rooms in Beak Street. St Denis ran a course for actors who were already working; we paid something like £1 a week and you could go and rehearse and act scenes from a play or do various exercises – you know, the usual thing one had done at drama school (rubbishy one, I went to). I remember rehearsing the first act of *The Cherry Orchard* and Marius Goring was playing Epihodov. Very early on there's a line where he is complaining about his boots squeaking. It was going all right, when Michel said, 'But Marius, I don't hear your boots squeaking', and Marius said, 'Well, I'm wearing sneakers,' or whatever we wore in those days. Michel said, 'But you must make me *hear* them squeak.' And he got up, and said 'I'll show you what I mean,' and showed how by the pressure, the way you say that your boot squeaks, and the way your foot moves and the way you listen to that, we get the feeling that your boots squeak although there's no sound at all; and he was dead right. It was in that sort of area that he opened up a kind of new horizon.

What was Komisarjevsky like?

Well, I only played a tiny tiny part in a super production he did of *The Seagull*, with Edith Evans, and understudied Konstantin. I never got to know Komisarjevsky at all, but he was an adventurous, mad sort of conceptual director. He could also be very realistic, as he was with us, but there again he was a person who stimulated actors' imaginations. I don't necessarily believe in directors as such, I mean it's nice to have someone whom you can trust, one to share your opinion with – someone like that can be a friend. It's useful if it's a director you know who can pull you down, but above all, particularly when you're young, someone who can make the world that much larger for you, point out something you hadn't thought of or dared. It's enabling you to dare that is where they can help, as well as keeping a disciplined eye out to see that things don't get sloppy.

I remember something Komisarjevsky said – funnily enough it was to do with the foot again. In *The Seagull*, after they've been sitting for a long time, Masha gets up and says, 'My leg's gone to sleep', or words to that effect. Martita Hunt was playing Masha, and Komisarjevsky said, 'No, Martita, it's no good just getting up, saying your leg's gone to sleep and stumbling awkwardly. It means something quite different. It's your excuse: you are drunk, and you must somehow let us know you are drunk when you say, "My leg's gone to sleep," although we haven't seen you drink.' And it revolutionised the thing for her.

What is an actor doing, do you think, when he is speaking badly,
whether in Shakespeare or not? What is bad speaking?

Well, it's sloppy, isn't it? It's something that doesn't hold your interest, but that can be the acting as well as the speaking. It's very difficult to separate the two. For me, the English language is basically iambic pentameter. That's our natural rhythm. So often you hear people in the street speaking in iambic pentameter and wish you could inform them of the fact. There must be a sort of natural, native move that way, and one should respect it without becoming its slave; but to treat it as dirt, of no use to you, is sacrilege. Gielgud's voice was glorious, it was a thrilling instrument, but too many people told him so. I don't mean out of vanity, because he's a man of absolutely no vanity at all, but he began to listen to it, and that became painful, it became rich and vibrato, and the words became meaningless, in a way. When I played Hamlet in 1938 in modern dress, he came to see it and wrote me a long letter afterwards, a very sweet letter, almost every word of which I can still remember, needless to say. He said, 'You must work at the beautiful execution of words', and I thought, 'No, fuck that, that's the last thing I want to do.' If you're speaking correct English, I don't want to put every word in a jewel case. It can be fascinating for two minutes or so, but it's not what it's about. The beauty of words is nothing to do with oneself; there's the writer, the language, the whole thing about carrying on.

So that was one of the times when I began to resist, and that led me into trying to find a hair's-breadth stop on a line. I didn't know till a long time later, because he was younger than I am, that Alan Badel did the same thing, and he indeed may have reacted in the same way. I discussed it donkeys' years ago with Peggy Ashcroft, who was a dear and very close friend, and she was violently opposed to it. For me, although Peggy certainly doesn't listen to her own voice, there is quite a splurge of beauty going on, do you know what I mean? She's a very close friend of George Rylands [1902–99], who speaks verse beautifully, and I think she takes her thing from him. On the other hand, perhaps 30 years ago, he heard me reading some Milton on radio and wrote me a sweet note saying, 'Thank God, at last someone has realised that if you read Milton, you've got to put the stop at the end of every line and you've got to mark that *caesura.'* So I will still use my stop because very often I think it clarifies, or makes it easier for an audience to understand what's passing. When I played Shylock a couple of years ago I did it. Now and then my own ear will fail, or my own rhythm will go wobbly, but I like to know that I can do it even if I discard it, so long as it doesn't impede the emotion or the sense. I have a sister-in-law who works in France a great deal, directing small things, and she was aware that I did this slight stop thing. Last year she was doing something with some students in France and told them, 'Well, my brother-in-law does this.' She said to me, 'I never realised how it so often made the sense.' Only in a tiny way – you just give it a little flick.

When I started in the theatre, the relationship with the older actors, the generation before me, was very different to what it is these days. They were people who didn't speak to small-part actors, but would all insist that, if you were feeding the leading part, every line ended *up*. Now, I found this torture to do and artificial. I know what they meant: they didn't want to be having to pick things off the ground. But the poor sods who came on were always having to feed it *up* to them and I very often wouldn't because I thought this was against my own thing. Now I find that the thing is *down*, and this depresses me so much.

This is the latest trend in verse-speaking, isn't it, in the last 20 years or so?

It grates on my ear. It isn't just verse, it's speaking in the street, on the radio, everything is on a down beat. It goes with a sort of attitude to life, it never seems to lift speech, make life seem brighter. Maybe the going up thing was equally irritating, not depressing, but irritating to people, and there must be a sort of balance in the throw. The other day I was thinking I'm sure that everything in life really only makes sense if it's got a kind of rhythm, if there's a rhythm to what you do, and how you speak, and how you cope with things. I think if I had a funny little drama school that's what I would do, what I would settle for, to make sure all the pupils dance, move, speak, do something on a rhythm. Purely to get the thing flowing. Am I talking rubbish?

Is there a great difference in approach between speaking prose and verse?

I don't think there should be. As far as Shakespeare is concerned, he wrote infinitely more prose than people think – they always think everything's in verse. But my goodness that prose has wonderful rhythm to it, I mean it's actor's stuff to speak, isn't it? Whether it was a deliberate mark for people to notice, or not, I don't know, but I like to think there's maybe a different tone for speaking prose. I can't think of a single example, but maybe when you're carrying on in some splendid piece in iambic pentameter, there's a slight shock at the change of rhythm into prose, at the change of attitude.

Do you think there's been a change in the standard of speaking in the theatre? A deterioration?

I fear so, yes, I do feel that. There are some lovely exceptions, you know.

What do you think is the difference in the driving force behind actors now?

I really wouldn't know, I'm afraid. I mean, we've all been ambitious, but maybe it was that there was no social security when I was a young actor, nothing to fall back on. If you hadn't got work and you hadn't got private means – I mean I would live for a day on that bun I just ate. Maybe it was very healthy. I was supposed to be two years at drama school but I couldn't take it after six months. My fellow students used to bring me sandwiches and things like that. I thought I've got to do something, not just rely on other people for food.

I think maybe the ambition for success is still there, but maybe the ambition to be a classical actor has disappeared. I don't know why that has happened.

TV has obviously made a huge difference. I've found it a bit depressing when I've been involved in casting, when you think someone at an audition would be good, and they say, 'Sorry but I'd rather hang on and hope that a TV crops up in a month's time.' I thought we all wanted to be on the stage. Some people are mad to be in films, but the basic thing is theatre and having your feet on boards. That's basic to everything because that's the only form that goes back many thousands of years.

ALEC GUINNESS

Unfortunately what's happened as well is that very often theatre plays are cast from television success.

This is a new horror, and it doesn't work, it never has worked, when they cast so-called film stars in plays. If they do work, it's to do with the film star actually being a perfectly decent accomplished stage actor before, who knew what he was doing.

Are there any disciplines in the speaking of either verse or prose that you would like to see generally applied?

As I have said, I have no general principles really, other than that I am sure that rhythm is important and making sense so that you don't have to spend hours explaining what you're saying to an audience. It isn't so much verse-speaking, but I find that my chief bugbear in life generally at the moment is false emphasis. I catch a train from Waterloo and I hear an asinine girl's voice saying 'The three-EIGHTeen FOR Bournemouth WILL leave from platform…' and you're in doubt immediately. Did she think it wasn't going to leave and they changed the platform? It seems so simple to leave things alone and let the verb tell the story, which is what it does. I wrote a silly book last year, a kind of semi-autobiography, and I think the only time I touch on that sort of thing is, when I was trying to get a scholarship to RADA and I went to Martita Hunt, whom I didn't know. She was a very civilised, cultured woman, and she had very very good taste in things theatrical. I used to have to read stuff to her, and it was she who said, 'For God's sake make sure you've got hold of the verb, let the nouns more or less take care of themselves, and totally ignore adjectives and adverbs.' A rule of thumb, not meant to be taken absolutely literally of course, but it is a basic thing. When I questioned her, she said, 'Well, the verb is the driving force of a sentence.' If you've got that you're halfway home, and never, unless the sense shouts for it, give any emphasis to a personal pronoun. I hate rules, but that is really the only one that I have, and of course I'm happy to break it for character purposes.

Are there other actors you can think of, past or present, whose speaking you admire?

As well as Sarah Badel, Jill Balcon speaks with perfection. There are some actors from the past, who must have made recordings. Robert Speaight [1904–76] was not a particularly good actor, I don't think, but a very interesting man and he gave it up and drifted away, and wrote. But I can still hear him, as Ulysses in *Troilus and Cressida*, in a production at the Westminster Theatre. It made me think I wanted to play that, and I've wanted to play it ever since. It's too late now, but I regret not having played that, except that I would have been reproducing in some way or other what Speaight did. He was wonderfully controlled, authoritative, perfectly light, not ponderous at all but wonderfully incisive speech, like a splendid aria.

Leon Quartermaine [1876–1967] was another old actor who I think went too far. He was a beautiful actor and I adored him, but as he got older, he became more and more fanatical about it. He would stand or sit in the wings when other actors were on, wincing all the time at the false emphases, or lack of something, but acutely aware.

What size do you think a company should ideally be?

I don't know where I picked it up from, some learned work probably, but I believe that Shakespeare's own company was a *compagnie de quinze* – fifteen actors, and odds and sods were brought in to swell a scene as required. It's a very good number, fifteen. St Denis' company was fifteen and they could hang around together for five, six, seven years. By then, everyone's fucked everyone, and some will break away, psychologically.

I just want to go back to that rule of thumb you mentioned about the verb driving the sentence, and ignoring adjectives...

Nearly always ignore them. The noun will pretty well take care of itself because that's what the sentence is going to be about. 'I bought a house in the country' You're going to get *bought, house, country,* and then *I,* and *in the.* So you get a little picture. There's a kind of vulgarity if you put emphasis on adjectives, unless it requires it for the sense. You know, 'I've got a *blue* picture on the wall, and a *red* one in the bank.' You've got to emphasise them if you're pointing something up. But I wouldn't take a sentence apart like that unless I was in difficulty.

How important are vowels in speaking?

I would have thought vowels and consonants are equally important. My own tastes are fairly catholic, and I like regional accents. What makes me feel ill is this Bonham-Carter English, currently to be seen in *A Room with a View*, this Sloane Street cockney. I love cockney, but I hate that kind of mangled mid-Atlantic speech that's trying to let people know you're frightfully grand because you can afford to be sort of sloppy. The vowels have all gone. I hate that. If I get into trouble with a word, I take out the Oxford English Dictionary and see what they say. I know that some people don't swear by the Oxford and complain about it, but it does remind you that there are pure vowels and there are impure vowels, and an enormous number of variations. Something caught my eye this afternoon, just before you came, not in the Oxford Dictionary, but in Fowler's English. My eye fell on the word that we use for a small platform on which you stand – *dais*. I think I've always said *da-is*, but that would have been right out. They happen to quote the OED on it, saying that the correct pronunciation is *dace*. Well all right, I've learnt something today. I must have said 'dais' dozens of times in my life for one reason or another, but now I shall remember to say, 'He was standing on a dace', and no one will know what I'm talking about.

What about the importance of breath in speaking?

Well, I've got no breath left at all now. I used to work very hard, under Guthrie and all those people who used to teach one those things, but I don't think I really paid a lot of attention to anything. I never had any vocal trouble. I used consciously to take a breath where it seemed possible to sustain a kind of sound, and the flow of a line through, but with age it becomes more and more restrictive. I think these things come naturally, on the whole, don't they? Unless you stop and get puzzled, and then you get into a huge muddle – 'God, where shall I get that breath?'

Have you ever found a genuine need to say five lines in one breath?

No, absolutely not, this was purely because Tony Guthrie said you ought to be able to. But I would try it to see if I could, and one could, just, but the effort and the concentration required, and as for what the five lines were... Oh no, I wouldn't recommend it to anyone, except that to have breath control, as singers obviously do, must be a very useful thing, and always to have a little bit of breath left over, so you don't get stuck if something happens.

Talking of opera singers – how important is variation of tone?

Oh, I'm sure it's enormously important. I just droned on the same old way forever.

I get the impression that what you are driving at is that if you are as much in touch with yourself as possible, that's all that is important.

No, I'm not sure. If I were starting again now, I would go to a singing teacher, not because I want to sing, but I'm very aware of that lack in myself. A great god for me was T S Eliot. All my tests in reading literature and poetry are very much centred around Eliot. It's a very uninflected line, you know. The line is very even-paced; that's what gave it its kind of modernity, I think.

This might seem a bit obvious, but how important is audibility?

Oh, it's totally important. I don't see any excuse. I mean, there are thousands of excuses, but everything should be done to overcome them because the poor bloody playwright's written something and an audience loses interest if they don't hear you. They begin to lean back and drift away. Whatever the difficulties the actor must go through, he should sacrifice for the sake of author, other players, audience, to be audible. All right, it's going to be too loud sometimes, and he will learn how to measure that in time, but in my reckoning – maybe I'm wrong, particularly after my experience last night – but in my reckoning nearly all good actors are audible. Another thing of course to do with audibility is the lighting. People think they can't hear if they can't see. We went through a phase of a lot of obscure lighting, and audibility seemed to go out of the window at the same time, but the moment the eyes and face are visible, and you can see a mouth working, the words are easier to catch.

How do you reconcile the actor's personal need for expressiveness with the classical demands of the text?

Everyone works in different ways and I don't know how you work, but when you read for the first time a play which you know you're going to be involved in, you can't read it totally coldly, at least I can't. Already I'm in a hat and a wig, and whatever it may be. There's an involvement the actor cannot escape once he knows that's his sentence for the next however many months to come. You are already in that and you will find the character, or fail to find it, with time. It probably goes through various variations, and side by side with that you've got to pay respect to the whole. It should be a happy marriage of which you are unaware that there is any division. How one does it, I don't know.

Who, in your experience, can be imitated without being a bad influence?

I think to imitate anyone is a bad influence to start with. In some ways I think you can learn more from watching bad actors than good, because a good actor totally deceives you, and you don't really know how it's done. I went a few weeks ago to see Maggie Smith in *Interpreters* [by Ronald Harwood], but in a way she was too good. By the second act I felt I'm not particularly interested in this play. I don't think it's all that good, and you're being marvellous, but I cannot put a finger onto where you're acting. I was so fascinated by Maggie's impenetrable acting. I mean, she was there, it was absolutely making me laugh, making me serious, on the flow. I was entirely in her hands, and I couldn't detect it. You know if the worse comes to the worst you can watch someone's feet and think, 'You've got to move that now, haven't you, because you're nearly off balance,' or, 'You've stood there too long.' It should surely be like some wonderful make-believe that convinces you. I think imagination is the most important element in it all. Imagine yourself into a situation, imagine yourself in command of a thousand people. It's a funny, funny business and I don't know why we all do it, except that it's fascinating.

I'd just like to ask one more question. It concerns the period you spent with John Gielgud in the thirties. It is remembered by theatre historians as a golden period, and I wondered what it was actually like to function in a company like that. Was there anything that

prevented you at times from performing? What would prevent you
from giving of your best?

I haven't a clue. One thought one was giving one's best, and one was also sensible that it was very limited and very little was required of you – a few lines here and there every night. I think he was torture as a director: 'Come on from the left! Come on! No, no, no, the other left!' Always last-minute changes, and this stiffness, and social hierarchy. Disgruntled actors used to say you only got jobs if you went to parties, met the right people. I don't think that was so myself. Certainly not in my experience because I didn't go to parties, but I got work. I think there were some people around who spotted some odd kind of talent which interested them. Even when I was playing in Guthrie's production (the very worst he ever did) of *The School for Scandal*, in 1937, someone like Angela Baddeley would speak to me because I was chummy with Glen Byam Shaw who was her husband, and I was playing Lorenzo or something. But other people in that sort of range weren't noticed. I was in two productions with Edith Evans before she spoke to me. I didn't resent it at all; I would hold the door for her endlessly, and not even a 'Good evening'. But when she did speak to me it was a memorable occasion. It was during a night rehearsal of *The Seagull*, at what is now the Albery Theatre and used to be the New [now renamed the Noël Coward Theatre]. It was a lovely theatre to play in and the cast was scattered around in distant bits of the stalls, you know, ten o'clock at night after a whole day's rehearsal. Peggy Ashcroft and Stephen Haggard, who were playing Nina and Konstantin, were in some sort of turmoil on stage. I think I must have dozed off a bit, it went on so long, with Komisarjevsky trying to explain and being very Russian. I was sitting by myself, about two rows behind Edith, who I thought a great actress. I could tell from the turn of her head that she thought she'd spotted whatever the difficulty was and wished to communicate it, but she didn't want to stop the rehearsal. It wasn't her business to interfere, so she wanted to find someone to tell it to, and she found me, two rows behind her. She said, 'You see young man,' and she lowered her voice, 'You see young man, it's all a great big glass tube, and you blow down it.' And she sat back, well satisfied with what she'd said. It was absolutely mad, but I sort of knew what she meant: that you must have some technical accomplishment and give breath through it, it was the glass of the invisible.

She didn't speak to me again for about another six weeks or two months. Then I got promoted, because there was a shift in the cast, to playing the part of Yakov, the butler, about five or six lines at the most. It had been played by the Assistant Stage Manager – nice chap but I knew he wasn't an actor; I had that horrible feeling – I've never been jealous in my life but I just thought, It's not quite right: he's not an actor and I am. I was very very young. Anyway, I got pushed into doing this part. Komisarjevsky had arranged things very well, and there was a particular exit line where there was a laugh, a perfectly legitimate absolutely true line which got a nice laugh, and that was it. On the first night that I went on, it brought the house down, I mean it was a huge round of applause, which went straight to my young head. I thought, 'I knew it!' I didn't mean it vengefully, but I just thought, 'That's OK.' Edith used to be sitting in the wings on a hamper at that moment, and I flicked the line and looked past to her, and it had registered. There was a gracious smile and a nod of the head, and I was cock-a-hoop. The next night, there was no laugh, there was nothing at all. It was the most dead dead silence, and I thought, 'What did I do? I didn't do anything different.' That went on for two or three nights – the whole thing had gone – and then Edith beckoned me over and said, 'You've lost that laugh', and I said, 'Yes, what am I doing? I don't understand what it is.' And she said, 'But you didn't know how you got it in the first place.' And I thought, well, that's true. But she said, 'You're not to worry. Don't worry about it. It will take you about a week, and when you've found it again in about a week's time, it's there for ever.' And I said, 'Well, what makes you say that? I haven't got that confidence.' And she said, 'Oh, I know because it's natural to you to seek a laugh, but if ever you strive for a laugh, it will elude you. It's simply not in your make-up. But your natural gift that way will emerge and the next time it happens, just remember what the feeling was and always reproduce that.' And it was absolutely so. A week to the day, there I was happily back with my big laugh, not quite knowing how I got it, but knowing that at least I was relaxed about it and not caught up with feeling there's a big laugh coming, or timing it in a conniving way with the audience.

And one more question – how did you find approaching Hamlet?

It was tricky for me because I'd been in Gielgud's *Hamlet* at the New Theatre, and I was in Olivier's *Hamlet* and understudied him, and I'd seen various other Hamlets, and they were all different. The greatest by far was Ernest Milton [1890–1974], which is probably a name you've never even heard of. Eccentric, he became very eccentric. He was a dear man, an American, born in San Francisco, and he was Sybil Thorndike's leading man at the Old Vic. Physically in many ways very affected. He spoke beautifully but the voice was affected, or the way he said words. It was an astonishing experience, that particular *Hamlet*, only on for two performances, I think, at Sadler's Wells. I was struck dumb. I had to go back to bed and stay there for 24 hours; I couldn't speak to anyone. That's the greatest performance I've ever seen. I don't know what it was – some of it was ridiculous, funny, he was absurd, but you were in the presence of something which you thought Shakespeare would have approved. It was new-minted, beautifully enunciated. In a way philosophically he was like a bombshell, but all those things like 'what a piece of work is a man', 'quintessence of dust', all those things had an explosive quality, as if the Renaissance was just happening. It was a new birth of ideas; it was suddenly a play of absolutely new, fresh and exciting ideas. The tears were pouring down my face all the time. It was like being in on some strange, wonderful birth. When it came to playing my first Hamlet, Guthrie directed and it was a wonderful production, but I think awfully ersatz tones of Gielgud kept coming through, without his magic voice. I'd got married six months before, and as part of our honeymoon we spent a week with Tony Guthrie at his house in County Monaghan. We wanted to talk about *Hamlet* and a few mornings we went up to some old playroom he had had as a child and I would do bits of the soliloquies. I think there was only one original thing, which just kind of happened because I felt it that way. That was in the scene with Ophelia, the 'Nymph in thy orisons…' scene. Until then, any production I'd seen had always had some tip-off that Claudius and Polonius were hearing the whole thing. You know, there was either a hand seen behind the curtain, or some bit of business. I said to Tony, I see no reason for any business, because it surely isn't possible that he doesn't know they're there. It's just such a strange situation for her to be there, alone, unprotected, vulnerable. It worked very well, but I don't think I contributed anything more.

I did it again in 1951, which was the famous disaster, again at the New Theatre. Guthrie had been very under the influence of Jung and Freud, and the psychoanalyst Ernest Jones had a tremendous influence. Secret talks went on about what it was all about. So in 1951, when I was getting a bit old for it, I think I'd rejected all that, but I was very influenced by a Spanish philosopher called Madariaga who lived in England and who wrote a book about Hamlet. I don't know whether I could read it now, but at the time I thought it was fascinating. He made the statement that, in the same way that we are now so much under the influence of America, in Shakespeare's time the world empire was Spain. I went all Elizabethan/ Spanish. I employed a marvellous Spanish designer, but there were a thousand things wrong with it. One of the things I've always regretted not doing – I don't think I hate anyone, but I would love to have made a public speech in dispraise of Harold Hobson [1904–92, theatre critic of *The Sunday Times*]. The production had a functionally ghastly first night. It was the first electronic lighting board used in this country, and every other cue went wrong. Each time I moved to the wings to say to the stage manager, 'Bring the curtain down, I'll go and make a speech: Money back, go home', everything came right again. So you thought, 'Ah, well, now we're all right.' Five minutes later, the whole thing again. Total madness and horror. The cast were marvellously sweet, but Hobson said in his review, 'With the exception of Alec Guinness, we will never hear of any of these actors again.' Now, I had cast the play, and among the actors he was never going to hear of again were Stanley Holloway, Michael Gough, Robert Shaw, Alan Webb… In fact, with the exception of the mistake I made with the man who played the Ghost (a New Zealander with a very good voice, but no use, and one should have said Goodbye to him), and the totally insane Ophelia (I'd chosen her madness and that was a big mistake, but she was also very pretty). Apart from those two, every single member of that cast has starred either in Hollywood, London, or on TV. The effrontery to say that…! I'd made the mistake of sharing the production with Frank Hauser, who I didn't know well but he had directed me in a radio play. I was very impressed with his ear and thought he'd be very good at keeping me on the mark and making sure I was making sense and not listening to myself.

I directed the first two weeks of it and then withdrew, and well, I'm afraid the rest of the cast didn't trust Frank particularly. I'm not blaming him, but it was divided and a bit of a mess. We didn't quarrel, we saw eye to eye on things, but it just became a mess, I'm afraid.

Was it very tiring for you, playing Hamlet?

Well, all the great tragic, rip-roaring parts have a twenty-minute break before the final fling, and with the shortened version, that gets cut down. The first time I did it, it was absolutely every word in the Folio, and was about four hours and ten minutes. We would start at one o'clock on matinee days – only Saturday matinees, I couldn't cope with eight a week. One was young and had the stamina. But it is easier on the long stretch, and it has a sort of greater importance, too, somehow. Guthrie did a wonderful job, very exciting. He used all sorts of bold things. The graveyard scene was done entirely in the rain with umbrellas up, for instance. Although the press wrote things like 'This *Hamlet* with cigarettes and cocktails…' it was absolutely classical in its movement, in its speech.

REX HARRISON

*Were you influenced by a particular teacher, director or colleague at
an early stage?*

Well, I went on the stage when I was 16 at the local rep. I didn't get a vast
amount of training there because I was just understudying and watching.
I came to London in the middle to late '20s and went to the theatre a lot
and was influenced enormously by the naturalism of Gerald du Maurier,
Charles Hawtrey, Ronald Squire, etcetera, and it stayed with me. I've
always believed in truth and naturalism in acting, and the fourth wall, and
keeping it inside your head. Those actors were rather masterful at that,
and I used to love the way they got their comedy – it was so easy and
intensely naturalistic. That's rather stuck with me all through my career:
whatever I've done I've tried to bring to it a form of naturalism.

Were they un-physical actors?

Yes, in the sense that they didn't move about a lot. They had rather fine
voices and quite big ranges and they managed to move an audience to
tears, without – which is always fatal, isn't it? – shedding a tear themselves.
This was part of their mystique and magic. In *My Fair Lady* for instance,
'I've Grown Accustomed to Her Face', which does finish in an emotional
manner, I was always terribly careful not to move myself but to move the
audience. I think this applies to all forms of acting really.

*So when you were creating that part, did you aim to consciously pitch
your voice in such a way, or did you start with the truth of the feeling
of the thing?*

Well, I've always believed in this old-fashioned thing about the recognition
scene in plays. There's always, somewhere, a recognition scene, where
the audience and the actor at the same time recognise some truth. I

Rex Harrison in Noël Coward's *Design for Living*, Savoy Theatre, 1939, with Diana Wynyard
(Mander & Mitchenson Theatre Collection)

think that, provided Higgins was played the correct way all through the piece, as Shaw intended him to be, then the fact that he suddenly realises that he has fallen in love with Eliza irrevocably is a terrible blow, and his recognition scene is that number. He comes on, suddenly having realised this terrible thing (because he is a confirmed bachelor and thinks it would never happen to him). What you have to do with the audience then is to push the emotion through the number, without moving yourself.

They say that you created a new way of singing in that part...

That was a piece of luck in fact. They came over and asked me to do it, and they hadn't got many of the songs written at this point. They said, 'The thing is, we must know who's going to play Higgins because how we construct the songs depends on who's going to play it.' I couldn't make up my mind at all. I kept sitting around in Claridges for about six weeks not quite making up my mind. Then I said, 'Let me try and see what I can do with my voice.' So I went to Wigmore Street where there is a singing teacher who tried to produce my baritone voice as best he could. I was singing out of his windows, trying to hit the houses across the street. I knew it was never going to work. I was going to be a lousy baritone, that's all. So I rang Lerner and told him I didn't think I could do it. He said, 'There's a fellow in London who is conducting in the pit at the Coliseum and he may be able to help you because he's been there a long time and has seen people dealing with numbers like patter songs.' His name was Bill Lowe. He came over and I had a piano brought in, and he taught me in a few easy lessons how to speak on pitch. It's not that easy because you have to be very musical. You have to be able to hit the note right in the middle. Strangely enough, when I'd played it for two years or so at the Lane, and two years in New York, when I was tired at the end of a week I would find that the most non-tiring thing was to try and vocalise it.

Which means you actually sing it?

Yes, which I occasionally did on Saturday nights because it was sort of easier.

And were you a good baritone?

No. I was lousy, but at least I wasn't struggling. I would always find myself at odds with the conductor. I mean they were all wonderful, but it was difficult for them because I never looked at them. Most singers wait for the down beat, you know, but I'd like to wait for the orchestra to start and then catch them up. It wasn't a method conductors were used to handling.

So that happy accident you just described – not wanting to be a poor baritone and meeting Bill Lowe – was perhaps a culmination of something you may have been doing all through your acting life. You have a wonderfully melodious speaking voice…

But I hadn't thought of it in those terms. I was never conscious of it until I had a melody underneath it. I wanted it to be an extension of Shaw's words into the song, and I think it worked very well, but I never thought of it before. When you're playing parts, you don't think of melodies, do you?

That's part of what we are trying to discover…

Phrasing of sentences and lines and punctuation is something which one learns by trial and error and being relaxed and loose in front of an audience. I try and keep myself amused by varying the phrasing. But you don't get much chance of doing your own original phrasing with Shaw, do you? He sticks you with this marvellous prose which has a sort of rhythm and a metre that has to be stuck with. I found when I played Shotover in *Heartbreak House* recently, one has to more or less set a mould and stay with it. If you try fooling around or breaking Shaw up, he doesn't work.

That's interesting. One of the things Peter Gill told me to ask was whether it's possible to get a laugh on your own in Shaw, and you've just answered the question, which is that you and Shaw do it together.

Absolutely. You can with people like Freddy Lonsdale [playwright, 1881–1954]. You can more or less choose your own phrasing and maybe get a laugh somewhere and lose it somewhere else. I was a great admirer of A E Matthews [1869–1960]. I remember years ago being in a play with him, playing a small part, and I used to stand in the wings and watch Matty, as he was called. I couldn't believe it, he would lose an obvious laugh that he had had the night before, and then try something totally different the next night. He was always playing around with it.

You said you have to be free and relaxed in front of the audience, and that's how you find out how you can vary your phrasing. How do you relax? Do you have an exercise or something you do beforehand?

No, no, I don't. Even in a long run I'm always a little 'tight' before I go on stage. One is energising oneself purposely. To open a door and walk on stage is always a hazard. It's never not been a hazard. So that perhaps forces one to disguise it in what is after all only a form of naturalism. It's not being totally naturalistic, but it appears natural. And of course the other thing about playing comedy in the theatre is to appear not even to know the audience are there. The moment they start to be there, you may be in trouble. I dare say that's a style of acting which has been replaced. Where did this new style of director-ridden theatre happen?

Well, I guess it came originally from cinema, wouldn't you? I mean, it may have started with Stanislavsky and people like that, and they may have influenced others. But I think their power probably rose with the movies when the director was all-powerful. And gradually that came across to television and now it's been subsumed by certain so-called intellectual theatre directors. Do you not like it, the directorial theatre?

No. It's like the way I don't like actors playing to an audience. I don't like to see the backstage. I like to see curtains going up and down. It's a sort of workshop feeling that I don't think has much to do with the theatre.

It may be that people doing those things are reacting against a form of theatre. Did you feel when you saw du Maurier that he was a sort of revolutionary actor compared with the old barnstormers?

Certainly, and what's fascinating is that when I first came to London in the twenties, there was no Shakespeare being played in London. At the Old Vic there probably was, but most of the companies, like Frank Benson's [F R Benson, 1858–1939], would be on the road. I think people like Olivier brought the Bard back to popularity. And I agree that the Hawtreys and du Mauriers were a great breakaway from declamatory acting.

You didn't care for that style?

I watched those touring companies in Liverpool, and the acting was very mannered and declamatory. I didn't care for it, no. And I think if I had ever seen Shakespeare played as I saw it the other day, in a production of *Hamlet* with Kevin Klein, where he played with total naturalism and those soliloquies were absolutely spoken thoughts – then I might have wanted to play Shakespeare.

Why did you not want to play Shakespeare?

Well, it seemed to me that I'd be stuck in a way I didn't want to act. I know that Olivier made great efforts to bring in a form of naturalism.

Would you think he's a naturalistic actor?

No, not at all. He's a marked character actor. Ralph Richardson [1902–83] tried without success to play Shakespeare. His whole method of acting, which I admired enormously, was eccentric, although in a great form of truth. An actor I admire enormously who is acting in London at the moment is Peter O'Toole. I think he combines a lot of things I like: eccentricity, truth, naturalism, and he never seems to go totally overboard to me.

In The Apple Cart *which he's in now, does he, as you said earlier, get the laughs in Shaw by doing it with Shaw?*

Oh I think he's embroidering Shaw a little by doing some rather eccentric physical things. But it seems to me that he speaks Shaw very much along the traditional line that you have to. I've seen it twice. He's awfully good – not uneccentric but it has a marvellous ring of truth always.

I read somewhere that you never liked Tudor verse...

I was misquoted – I didn't know personally how to deal with the Tudor plays.

You couldn't see how to apply your form of naturalism?

I couldn't quite see how it could be done, although I never gave it a lot of thought, I must say, because I was very happy playing the moderns.

Who of your contemporaries were you influenced by?

I've talked about Ralph, but you see when somebody's a magician you can never learn much from them. You don't know how they do it. That's the point.

He gave a wonderful description of a play. He said, 'With a play, you are playing with time. The curtain goes up and the play begins and it's like a great stone and it's going to roll inevitably down the hill to the bottom of the valley and what you have to try and do is occasionally stop it.' And it doesn't sort of mean anything, except that it means everything. What do you think of Richard Burton as a speaker?

Marvellous voice. It's a little declamatory for my taste. Just a little bit 'back' like they used to be in those old road companies. In films he brought the whole thing down to a perfectly naturalistic level. I did a film with him once, *Staircase*, just the two of us, where I was with him eyeball to eyeball, and he really was an awfully good actor. But I think that in the theatre he was just a touch 'actor laddy'...

I'm very fascinated by the audiences here in England since I've been back. I'm watching the audiences as much as the plays, and they seem to sit there totally riveted, but don't appear to feel anything. It may be the plays I've seen. Travelling back and forth as I do and acting on both sides of the Atlantic, it's very interesting that there is a great difference between the audiences. I mean, English audiences go as part of their lives, but in America it seems such an event. They're on the whole a slightly livelier bunch to act to, and therefore more receptive. You must remember that in New York they're probably fifty per cent tourists, who have come in to New York for a week, rather than the New Yorkers who are much more sophisticated. I think the English audiences are highly intelligent and they go to the theatre as part of their lives, but they don't show any emotion.

Within your school of naturalism, does speaking still have to be done immaculately?

Immaculately. And everything has got to be sounded – finish your words and all that.

*Have you carefully chosen between films and the theatre because you
feel that to speak live in the theatre is a precious thing? Does that
sound fey?*

No, it doesn't sound fey at all. I hadn't quite thought of it like that, but I
know that when I have done a spell of filming, for my own sake and for my
own morale, I am always very anxious to get back into the theatre. Film-
making is boring and makes you lazy. You never have to extend yourself.
If you get three minutes a day in the can you're doing very well. The only
thing one learns, which doesn't help you a jot on the stage, is to be able
to think in front of a camera. Long speeches can be very gripping in the
theatre, but you're wasting your time doing that on screen. All the great
screen actors, like Gary Cooper, would go through their scripts and just
cut them down to a line or two. It was the look which mattered, not what
they said.

*So maybe the movies have contributed to the decline, if there has been
one, in the ability of modern actors to deal with text.*

Maybe.

What do you think is meant by good speaking?

I think somebody speaking well is not overstressing any particular function
of the spoken word. I go back to my old hope for truth. Which is just say
it and think it and mean it, and it should come out all right.

*When you rehearse a speech the first time, do you know the perfect
way of saying it?*

No, it won't be the way it comes out.

So what happens?

Well, I think you have to find the character and make the lines fit the
character and fit yourself at the same time. It's a question of familiarising
yourself totally with the material, which really means going over and over
and over it until it becomes second nature. Then you're free to change
the phrasing and the emphasis if you wish, provided it's become part of
you. You have to do a lot of homework, you know. The rehearsal period is
frightfully beneficial, but I still think you have to take it home with you.

REX HARRISON   91

So you keep saying it over and over again?

Yes, in different ways, so that you get some shape.

Are you a Stanislavskyite?

Oh yes.

You know, you're a method actor, Rex.

Of course I am, yes. I draw on my own emotional experiences to do anything. We all do. I think that all good actors are naturalistic.

It's curious, a lot of people would think of you as belonging to a school of acting like Noël Coward, you give such an impression of ease. And yet underneath, not only do you work very hard, you actually use the terminology of Stanislavsky-based acting.

I think Noël Coward was a brilliant theatrical person, but I don't think he was a very good actor.

What about his speaking?

I didn't like it at all. It was too mannered for me. I know I do make it look easy, and of course it isn't, we all know that. But if I make it look so easy that people think I'm not doing anything...

Who among your younger contemporaries do you think speaks well?

Well, would you call O'Toole my younger contemporary? I think he deals with it very well. Albert Finney speaks well. He retains his native accent. If I kept my native accent I should be Liverpudlian.

Did you have a Liverpool accent?

No. My father was educated at Harrow. Younger contemporaries – well, another distinctly younger contemporary that I haven't seen a great deal of but what I have seen I like very much, is Alan Bates [1934–2003]. I think speaking well is something that one doesn't think about. If you start to think about speaking well, you may be lost.

Has there been a change in speaking in the theatre in your lifetime that you have observed?

Yes, it must have started in America. Whether they ever had a tradition of speaking quite like we did, I don't know, but the Brando grumble-and-grunt scratchy school started a vogue of blue-jean acting. From what I've seen since I've been here recently, the speech has got more sloppy.

If an actor is speaking badly, what is he doing?

Well, he's dropping the ends of his sentences, isn't he? Letting them go rather than following through. If you don't finish your words or if you don't keep the sentence afloat, that is bad speaking in my opinion. You may have a rising inflection or you may not. I think that was used very largely for comedy in the old days, which I don't think is necessary any more. I'm always absolutely fascinated when actors are really thinking it through the long arias, weighing how much time they can afford to take. I think it's a question of daring, but you have to have the material to dare with.

Have you acted in Restoration comedy?

I don't think so. I was put off Restoration, like I was put off Tudor verse, by the way it was acted. Then I would go to Paris and see the French actors playing Molière, which they do very much straighter than we do Restoration. I mean the play was always very funny, but with great normality. They don't have to have the handkerchief and the camp and the switch that we give our Restoration comedies, and which I dare say the Restoration actors didn't even give them.

What about the speaking of verse? Does end-stopping matter? Do you know what it is?

No.

Well you stop at the end of every line, in order to let people know that it's poetry, I suppose.

Well now, not if you're inventive you see. I've just seen Hamlet played by Kevin Kline in New York, who broke it up totally and it was wonderful. And he didn't give a damn where he stopped. He was thinking so hard it didn't matter.

And did it still have a kind of musical pulse throughout?

Probably not. But then I don't give a shit about the musical pulse you see. My theory is that you would be well advised, unless you are a genius, to stick to the rules. Then having once totally understood what the poet means, and so you are not purposely fucking him up, you can play around. But I think you have to do it straight first.

When you did the plays of Eliot...

Impossible to rephrase Eliot and Fry. You have to really stay with them. I don't think the technique you can use with modern naturalistic playwrights you can apply to verse in the same way. And anyway it probably sounds much better if you don't.

How do you handle vowels and consonants?

These are very highly technical questions. I mean if you're terribly conscious of vowels and consonants, how do you convey what I try to convey to an audience – that it's all so bloody easy?

But you have paid attention to them at some stage in your life, obviously.

Must have done. Must have done. Or I wouldn't have been heard in 62 years on the stage.

What about breathing?

Well you've got to be terribly conscious of it if you have to do anything of any length. I tell you what I learnt in *Fair Lady*: when you have fast lyrics you can do a thing called snatched breaths. I've only dealt with it once, but I was told that the snatched breath is something you can rely on. You don't have to fill your lungs with a huge amount of air before you start something. It's much better to take it during the line if you want it.

Do you do exercises?

No. I do yoga but that's not the voice. In a musical I used to do a few sort of *mmmmmmm* things, but I don't do an exercise. Actually I used to try and clear my throat on my first number.

ACTORS SPEAKING

That was your warm-up was it?

Yes. Specially in the afternoons.

What about variation of tone?

I suppose I am conscious of variation of tone because I wouldn't otherwise change it so much, but I don't think about it. One's terribly conscious of getting used to hitting the back wall. I've played in the most terrible big barns in my life, and tiny ones too, but you are conscious of being audible.

Do you have somebody go out there?

No no. You sort of sense it. I generally come and have a look at it with the house lights up. Don't have to do or say anything. Just my eye tells me what the 'throw' is. After that it's a question of degrees: how much you really want to go on there and enjoy yourself or whether you have to fight yourself to get on. I mean, I always have a bit of a struggle. I never want to go on stage and do it.

How do you feel when you get on there?

Oh, once I'm caught in my trap I feel slightly better. And better and better as the play progresses.

Is it the text that supports you or the audience, or what is it?

It depends entirely on how good the play is, doesn't it?

Who in your experience could be imitated without being a bad influence?

I don't think imitation is good anyway. I know that Olivier made Richard III a marvellous part of his life. It was an incredible performance and there hasn't really been a Richard since that I've seen, but I think it would be wrong for young actors not to try and find their own way round it and fight this great performance of the past. I think young people should be encouraged to be as individualistic as they can and worry it out their own way.

Patricia Hayes as Ruby in J B Priestley's *When We Are Married*, St Martin's Theatre, 1938, with Frank Pettingell (Mander & Mitchenson Theatre Collection)

PATRICIA HAYES

Were you influenced by a particular teacher, director, or colleague at
an early stage?

I was influenced by my mother. She was a teacher, and utterly obsessed
with people speaking well, with correct grammar. I was picked up on the
slightest grammatical error that I ever made. I don't think they teach
English grammar in schools now – French, German, Greek, but not English.
We were taught how to analyse, how to parse. Mother was a frustrated
actress, and she wasn't allowed to have anything whatever to do with show
business, dancing, nothing like that, it was taboo. So she made up her mind
that all her children were going on the stage, and in fact we all did, but I
was the first. I remember when I was five years old she said to me, 'I'm
going to teach you a beautiful poem called "The Lamplighter". It's about
a little boy looking out of the window and watching the lamplighter.' 'My
tea is nearly ready and the sun has left the sky' – it was all on those lines,
rather melodramatic, old fashioned style. She went through this poem
with me – I can see it clearly, in the kitchen of our house in Streatham.
When she got to the piece that goes: 'When I am older and can choose
what I shall do, Oh Leary I'll go round at night and light the lamps with
you', I burst into uncontrollable sobbing. She said, 'What's the matter?'
and I said, 'It's so sad, it's so sad.' Now what would make a very young
child aware of the hopelessness and the loneliness of that little boy? It
was the way my mother said it; she knew the power of words. Words
have, to me, far more power than music. Music affects you in a sort of
unphysical way, it's mental and spiritual and all that, but words have an
actual physical effect on you.

Have you been influenced by anybody else during your career as an
actress?

Yes. When I was very young we went to a teacher called Olive Richardson, and she did teach me a lot of recitations with which I would always go in and win the prize. When I was quite small, in fact, she taught me to say The Murder of Nancy from *Oliver Twist* by Charles Dickens. My mother took me away from her because she would keep teaching me cockney things and my mother hated that. The one disappointment for my mother, had she been alive when I got the award for *Edna The Inebriate Woman*, would have been that it was a cockney woman. 'Oh no,' she'd say, 'You've got such a beautiful speaking voice, why do these terrible cockney things?' But as far as I'm concerned it doesn't matter what dialect you're speaking.

No, it has to be good speech.

It does. Even more important if it's a dialect; people might not hear every word unless you're very careful. Then, when I first went to RADA (I went as a Juvenile; I was sixteen and went to school in the morning, RADA in the afternoon), there was a marvellous woman there called Miss McGraw. She used to give us an exercise where you took a huge deep breath and started speaking very high and descending – 'Do you mean to say that I could possibly go through the town telling every single person that I met that I could expect such a thing about you as that?' Then you'd start at the bottom and go up. She was marvellous, she made a great impression on me. I've always known the importance of having plenty of breath at the back of what I say from her. When we came back the next term there was no sign of Miss McGraw, and I asked what had happened to her. They said, 'We had to get rid of her, you know, because she had a very slight Australian accent.' She had of course, and today nobody would mind that. But they did. You could talk in a frightfully affected way but you couldn't have any sort of an accent. The theory was that you wouldn't get work unless you learnt to speak what they called the King's English. I think you should be able to talk any way you want, but when I hear myself now I'm horrified. I think, 'Crikey, I sound like the headmistress of Roedean.'

What do you think is meant by good speaking? If an actor is speaking well, what is he doing?

I think what is meant by good speaking is conveying the message in the way that the author intended it to be conveyed. It's as simple as that. The only reason for speaking indistinctly is if you were playing the part of a person who speaks indistinctly. That would make quite a funny character in a play, someone who from beginning to end nobody can hear. Otherwise there's no excuse, even if you're playing cockney. It's got to be distinct. Those old performers, like Marie Lloyd, they knew that it has to be very clear because you don't get the message across if they can't hear you.

Who among your younger contemporaries do you think speaks well?

Judi Dench. Brilliantly. Penelope Wilton – beautifully. There are plenty of people who speak well. I think that it is not only that they speak well but have an interesting voice, with plenty of light and shade. Patricia Routledge – I could listen to her whatever she's saying, whatever part she plays, because the voice has so much cadence in it, you see. It's wonderful to have a big range, and Judi Dench has that too. Janet Suzman. There's an endless number of them…

Have there been many changes in speaking in the theatre in your time?

Oh yes. Actually, on the whole I'd say that acting has got better. The first time I went to Stratford, in 1934, I was horrified at the standard of acting there, because they listened to their voices, they sang it. I said to one actor, 'Why do you say it like that?' He said, 'Well, Anthony Dull.' I said, 'I know, but why does he talk like that?' He said, 'Shakespeare called him Anthony Dull because he was a dull man.' So I said, 'Yes but you can be dull without being *Duuulll*.' I've always been fighting for people to use their voices in a more interesting way.

Without listening to the sound you make?

Oh, you can't listen to the sound, no, with Shakespeare in particular. He gives such wonderful opportunities for actors, because he gives you the line, tells you what the person is thinking and feeling. It's all there, like beautiful music with everything put in – how loud, how soft – yet there is still a freedom for characterisation. You can be any character you like, but it need never be dull or ponderous.

Would you approach the speaking of a classical text differently from a modern text?

No. I approach them both the same.

Is the approach different for comedy and tragedy?

No, except that I think there is a little bit of comedy in all tragedy, and there's a little bit of tragedy in all comedy. I've often thought I would love to play Lady Macbeth. Of course, I'll never play it now, but I used to think there's no reason why she shouldn't be a little like I am, and somewhere in there I'd find something to get a laugh. No person who is a truly human being has not got a side to themselves that is quite funny.

Is good speaking absolute or variable, be it in comedy, tragedy, classical and so on?

I think it's absolute. Yes.

Do you apply different rules to the speaking of prose and verse?

I don't apply different rules, but when I've got to speak verse it channels me into an area that I am not channelled into by prose. When you come to know it, subconsciously, the rhythm is there. You can't just keep playing about with the rhythms like you can with prose. That beat is there and it's rather like a musical accompaniment. The accompanist should follow you, but at the same time you have to be aware of the fact that they are there.

That's the verse?

Yes, to that extent I think I do apply a slightly different rule.

Which Shakespeare roles have you played, apart from Maria [in Twelfth Night*]? Have you played Rosalind?*

No! I've never played anything interesting really. Well, of course Maria was interesting. At RADA, when I was in the Juveniles I played Shylock and Cassius and Portia, and the funny thing is that I've never forgotten those long speeches. I have terrible difficulty now getting something new into my head. But once it's there you know it for ever.

*Are any of the technical things about verse-speaking important to you
– end-stopping, the caesura, feminine endings?*

I don't know what they are.

Rhyming couplets?

They're there, but you shouldn't emphasise them. I think you should
always go for the sense. The musicality that's inbuilt will always be there
if you speak it clearly and well and with the meaning at the back of it. I
think Shakespeare above all meant us to mean what we say.

What about vowels and consonants?

Well to some extent the vowel goes with the accent of the person that
you're portraying. But the consonant, whatever part you play, you should
really work at the consonants because how can you know what sense
you're making if they don't hear the t and the d and p and the b? They've
got to be there, not emphasised, but you should practise them.

*Who in your experience could be imitated without being a bad
influence?*

I think I might take a leaf out of Patricia Routledge's book. Certainly Judi
Dench is the most shining example, because whether she speaks soft or
loud, with accent or without, whether she's playing comedy or tragedy, to
me she is the tops. She's the greatest actor in this country today, in my
opinion. There are actors who really only want to be themselves, and then
there are other actors, in which category I put myself, who always want
to be someone else. I don't want to be me on stage, how boring that is. I
want to be somebody else. Surely that's why you take it up, to have this
opportunity to step into somebody else's psyche and skin.

MICHAEL HORDERN

Can we begin by discovering how you started as an actor?

As an appearer-on-stage I started as an amateur. As an actor, I probably started in the nursery, and I think we all do. Basically we're all children still playing charades. However, I did not become a professional actor until I was 25. I never went to a drama school or anything like that, but I was a very keen amateur and played in one or two very good amateur companies. I did some Shakespeare in the open air down in Hertfordshire where I was working. I joined the St Pancras People's Theatre, which was a sort of amateur Old Vic in a disused chapel in St Pancras, run by a marvellous woman called Edith Neville, who was a sort of amateur Lilian Baylis. We did repertory there all through the winter; it was bombed in the war and finished. But it never occurred to me that I would make a living from this larking about on the stage.

Until the age of 25, what were you doing?

I tried to be a schoolmaster to start with, because I couldn't think of anything better to do, but fortunately I got polio which put me out for about six months, and I was able to think better of it while I was lying flat on my back.

Has that left you with any side effects?

No, absolutely none. I was perfectly all right within six months. Then I joined a firm called the Educational Supply Association, which sold everything to schools: books, blackboards, you name it. It was during that time that I joined the amateur group in Hertfordshire, playing Shakespeare out of doors in the summer at various country houses. In the winter I did the St Pancras thing. I was a great friend of Christopher Hassall [1912–63], a poet, a very good actor, a man of parts. He wrote all the lyrics for

Michael Hordern in Tom Stoppard's *Jumpers*, National Theatre at the Old Vic, 1972,
and later in the Lyttelton (National Theatre Archive, Photo Zoë Dominic)

the Ivor Novello musicals at Drury Lane. We were at school together; we went to school, very very slowly, together. He went to Oxford, joined the OUDS, and played a quite memorable *Romeo and Juliet* with Peggy Ashcroft, which was brought up for several performances to what was then the New Theatre in London. He came to see me in some play at the St Pancras People's Theatre with somebody called Edward Marsh, and they said that they thought it might be a good idea if I tried to take it up professionally, which I did.

So whereabouts did you start professionally?

Well then, fortunately, there was a chap – now long since gone – with more money than sense, who was a fellow amateur actor in the company that used to do these Shakespeare seasons in Hertfordshire. He'd put some money into a play at the Savoy, at just about the time I was thinking perhaps I might try this, and he got me into this production as teaboy, third assistant stage manager, understudy, and all that. I left my exercise books on the Saturday and reported to the stage door at the Savoy on Monday, which of course one could do in those days – you can't now.

Did you actually appear on stage in any capacity at this point?

No, I didn't appear at all. I took my understudying very seriously and used to enjoy understudy rehearsals. Sometimes, when my principals weren't able to come, or had to go for a wig fitting or something, I would stand in for them and do my stuff. I think they were rather impressed that they had somebody who could actually do it. Among those interested in this production was Patrick Ide [theatre manager] who of course is still a power in the theatrical land. He took me under his wing and it is really to him that I owe my launch into the professional theatre.

How did he help from there on?

He got me to audition for a director called Ronald Kerr, well known in those days, who was directing three plays for the company for which Patrick Ide was manager, Westminster Productions. They were doing a tour of the capitals of Scandinavia and the Baltic with *Arms and the Man*, *Outward Bound* and Maugham's *The Circle*. Lovely engagement. I auditioned and was given the parts of Sergius in *Arms and the Man*, and

Henry in *Outward Bound*, one of the young lovers. And away we went to Oslo, Stockholm, Helsinki, Rega, Tallin, doing those plays – not a bad start, actually. When I got back, Pat Ide said, 'I think what you want really is a good dose of weekly rep. Now, I know Ronald Russell at the Little Theatre, Bristol, and I will recommend him to take you into the company.' He did, and I was there for two years, in 1937–38, and '38–39.

In retrospect, what is your opinion of weekly rep?

Well, a wonderful training. The hard way, for goodness sake. It taught me very few of the refinements of my craft (I was about to say art, but I'll say craft). But by God it taught me discipline, and it also turned me into a professional actor very quickly. I never cease, when I get a chance, to say thank you to Ronnie Russell, who is still happily living in Bristol. He doesn't direct any more, but often plays with the Old Vic. He and his wife Peggy Anne Wood [1912–98], they were wonderful. They ran this theatre with wonderful discipline. We did two 45-week seasons, although one was graciously given a week out every six or eight weeks, otherwise you were at it all the time, and that accounted for how many plays in two years? I don't know. Sixty or seventy.

You must have covered everything – classics and contemporary.

Yes. We didn't ever do any Shakespeare. I don't think I spoke any verse.

Why would that be? Because it wasn't commercial?

It wasn't commercial. You had to be commercial in weekly rep. Ronnie Russell was very brave. We did an Ibsen, we did a Shaw each season. We did Chekhov, and then of course we did all the West End successes one after another, drawing-room comedies and so on. Good mix. We even did the play I am concerned with now, *You Never Can Tell*. We did that in a week, and it was staggering, absolutely staggering.

Then you went and served in the war?

Yes, I was in the Navy.

How was it, trying to pick up your career after such an experience?

Well, I was very lucky because I was at sea pretty well all of my naval service. I suppose I was in uniform for four and a half years, all told, and my last appointment in the Navy was at the Admiralty. I was out in Ceylon, and I left there in the middle of 1944 to come home to a desk at the Admiralty. Before the war, while I was at Bristol, we had been used quite a bit by sound radio – BBC West – being the only professional actors in the area. So I was kind of friendly with the microphone. Not only that, but also some of the directors from before the war at Bristol had moved up to Broadcasting House. There I was, sitting at the Admiralty in an office job, and free on many evenings. Every other evening, we were allowed ashore, as we used to say, so I did a bit of moonlighting at the BBC, and did quite a bit of radio while still in uniform. Then, when I was demobilised in 1945, I was on the spot of course. For the first three years post-war, dear Broadcasting House paid the rent. I did a tremendous amount of sound radio and loved it. Love it still. It is a medium I very much enjoy working in. The sound of the voice, you see.

I'd agree with you there. And you must have covered the classics for the radio.

Yes, quite a bit of the classics, but also a very great deal of current affairs – what's it called? – features. And at that time, the first ten years after the war, sound radio was brimming with brains from the universities and brains from the services who had come back. Go off for your beer at lunch-time and you'd be having it with Dylan Thomas, Louis MacNeice – you name them. As I never went to a university or to a drama school, or any of that sort of higher education, it was really my university, those three years.

It must have changed your attitude towards acting?

Oh yes. I grew up, as it were. Yes, it was one of the turning points, looking back, of my career. Coming out after four or five years in the services and meeting this glut of brains.

Did you find many actors who hadn't served in the forces?

Quite a few, and there was quite a feeling at that time.

How were they regarded?

Some of them, frankly, not awfully well. I don't think anyone objected to anyone having been a conscientious objector, but there was quite a bit of sort of 'fringe' conscientious objecting, if you see what I mean, from not very good reasons. People had stayed in the profession and dug themselves in very happily, and they weren't awfully pleased to see some of us chaps coming back, taking off our uniforms, putting on our bowler hats and coming in and ousting them.

After the war, did you ever get ensconced in one theatre company again?

No, I didn't. I hopped from pillar to post, picking up commercial jobs.

Your main bread-and-butter was commercial theatre?

Yes. Fairly soon, television. I'm hopeless at remembering dates but it can't have been very long after the war that I played my first season at Stratford. I did do quite a bit of work at the Arts Theatre with Alec Clunes [1912–70], and that was the next big turning point, I think.

What sort of work went on at the Arts?

Oh it was very catholic. For instance, I played Ivanov in Chekhov's *Ivanov*. I played Old Paul Southman in a wonderful play, John Whiting's *Saint's Day*, which caused a tremendous theatrical furore, for one reason or another, which was jolly good for anyone who was in it of course – all the publicity. And Macduff to Alec Clunes' Macbeth. Those three plays, I suppose, did draw me to the attention of the critics and a few impresarios. Among them was Glen Byam Shaw, who was just about to take up his time at the Shakespeare Memorial Theatre in Stratford. Very bravely – because I had had almost nothing to do with Shakespeare – he offered me for the next season Caliban, Menenius in *Coriolanus*, Jaques in *As You Like It* and Sir Politick Would-be in *Volpone*. Not a bad little lot, but to me terrifying because I had no idea about any of them. I remember ringing up a girl who had been with us at Bristol and asking, 'What about this *Tempest*, this Caliban, who's he? Where do I go?' And she told me in no uncertain terms how lucky I was to be offered this. And the season turned out very well; it was a wonderful series of parts, and another turning point. One of the directors that season was Michael Benthall, who was about to take over the Old Vic. He booked me for the Old Vic the following year, where I had Prospero and King John. Richard Burton was my Caliban, and I think I was a better Caliban to Ralph Richardson's Prospero than Richard Burton was to mine.

After the initial fear of discovering that you had these four parts to play at Stratford, how did you fare? Did the fear dispel once you started working on them, or was it a struggle all the way through?

It was pretty terrifying, but I suppose every actor ought to be composed of fifty per cent confidence and fifty per cent humility. I think I had those things in roughly the right quantities, and it saw me through. I was of course terrified, particularly playing Menenius. I couldn't get the toffee-nosed patrician – not toffee-nosed, but aristocratic, jollying-on and despising the plebs at the same time, and absolutely confident in himself. I couldn't get the character, and Glen Byam Shaw, who was directing that play couldn't put me onto it somehow, you know how it is. At the first dress rehearsal he said, 'Come and have lunch with me. We'll go to the theatre restaurant.' And I said, 'Lovely, yes.' He bought the best bottle of claret they had, which wasn't bad, and I thought what an extraordinary thing to do to one of your actors who is just about to have to go down and put on his costume and play. And I went down, put on my costume, and that was the chap, that was him! It was a wonderful bit of psychology.

Did you have any problem getting to grips with Shakespeare?

No, I don't think I did, and I don't think that I ever have. It has seemed to me such marvellous good sense, and if you've got a sense of rhythm and know where the Ps, Ts, Vs and THs are, and you can see the words in your head, and you speak properly, there is nothing to be frightened of. I was never really frightened of speaking verse, and also I have always been a very quick study, even at school. If we were set ten lines of something to learn, I was always ahead of everybody else. I could learn very quickly and fortunately still can. That was a great help. I loved the verse, you know, and if you love it you can first of all see it in your mind while you are studying it. See the lines, and then, as you are rehearsing, the character takes over from the actor and there it is, all ready for you on first night.

So from Stratford to the Old Vic. Did you continue there for some time?

Can't remember. I think it was during that season I played Pastor Manders in – what's it called? Oh, come on, Ibsen's most famous play of all! – *Ghosts*. (This is me absolutely. My brain is going. I can still learn but I can't remember yesterday. I can fortunately remember my lines, which is a different part of the brain.) Yes, Pastor Manders in *Ghosts*, and the chap in *The Magistrate* by Pinero. Great fun.

So from now you were periodically visiting the Old Vic in between commercial engagements or television?

I haven't been in a commercial play in the West End – except for Alan Ayckbourn's first, *Relatively Speaking* – for something like thirty years until the present engagement at the Haymarket. It was all Old Vic and RSC, not only at Stratford but at the Aldwych.

We are coming into the fifties here. Looking back, was there anybody then who particularly influenced you?

I enjoyed working with various directors but they didn't have the personal impact of the ones I have mentioned: Ronald Russell first of all, Alec Clunes, Glen Byam Shaw. I enjoyed working with Michael Benthall and Robert Helpmann as directors. The directors on my real short list are much closer to today, much later in my professional career.

Who was running the Aldwych when you started working there?

Peter Hall. He was certainly an influence. I enjoyed working under him very much as a director. Peter Brook I did not enjoy.

Why would that be?

I found him, as I believe others don't, a dictator rather than a director.

Were there any actors who influenced you at all?

No, I don't think so. Being impressed by them, certainly. Enormously enjoying working with them, but I can't say that they have influenced me very much, and I'm rather grateful for that because I think if one is too influenced by an actor personally then you start to pick him up in your own work, which is a pity.

Of the actors you see at the moment, would there be anybody who impresses you with their verse-speaking?

I almost never go to the theatre! When I do, and hear verse spoken (I'm thinking of William Shakespeare), I am almost invariably disappointed. 'Oh, I wish I could be saying that,' I think to myself.

When you returned to Stratford to play Prospero in 1977–78, how had the structure of the company changed? I think there were various attempts to make it democratic, which is impossible as far as I can make out.

Yes, I think it's quite impossible. Over and over again one sees these companies being formed on a democratic basis, and they don't last more than a matter of weeks. All these battles go on, and it must be dreadful handing out the parts. No, not for me. Well, I don't think it was all that democratic that latest season at Stratford. It was not awfully happy. I suppose to start with, I was very much older and there was not the tremendous excitement there was the first season I was there with Ralph Richardson and Margaret Leighton. I mean, there were giants in those days. *The Tempest* is a great favourite of mine, and to find myself, as I was the last time, in a production which I did not really admire, and not awfully happy with the cast, was a sadness. In fact, I was so unhappy at the beginning of that season that I asked to be released from my contract.

Wouldn't they allow it?

Well, the letter never reached Trevor Nunn, I don't know what happened to it, but it didn't reach him until too late for any action to be taken. As I was contracted for the year to play Prospero, I was snared, if you like, into playing Don Armado in *Love's Labour's Lost*, and absolutely loved it. It was a lovely production, and it was heavenly to go into the theatre and be playing that. So in the end I was happy.

Did people offer advice on verse-speaking at this time?

Not to me, no. Not to me. I mean, if you are moderately well educated and moderately intelligent and you can read and speak English, verse-speaking seems to me absolutely instinctive. As long as you are speaking the verse of somebody who knows how to write it, like William Shakespeare, you can't go very far wrong.

Shortly after the war, I was a member of the Apollo Society, now defunct as far as I know. It used to give Sunday concerts, verse readings and music, all rather precious but good. We were watched over by the great Dadie [George] Rylands, and he was a great verse-speaker, very strict and disciplined about it. I wouldn't dare to criticise anybody as steeped in the English language as Dadie Rylands, but I don't think his verse-speaking would commend itself to today's actors. On the other hand, I wish to God that some of them could have a dose of Dadie Rylands, because I have seen some Shakespeare productions recently and been appalled by the non-sense of the speaking of some of the leading players.

Is there any particular classical production that stands out in your memory, from the time when you did go to the theatre regularly?

What a terrible thing to have to say – No! Gielgud's *Hamlet*, Richardson's *Peer Gynt*, Olivier's – what's the horror one? 'Enter Lavinia raped and with her hands cut off'? – *Titus Andronicus*. I remember that, but not for the verse-speaking. I would like to think I have seen a *Macbeth* that really took hold of me. I always think the next *Macbeth* I'm going to see is the one that will reveal the play, and I still haven't seen it. So I can't look back and say, 'Well there was that great *Macbeth*.'

Did you see Ian McKellen's?

Oh, I beg his pardon. Indeed I did. That is the best *Macbeth* I've seen, yes. Him and Judi [Dench]. I played it myself at the Old Vic.

How did that go?

Well, it wasn't as bad as some people think! I mean, everybody gets bad notices for Macbeth, but it always fills the theatre. If you're in trouble, put on *Macbeth* and they all come pouring in, and the notices are awful.

I mean everyone gets stinking notices for Macbeth, except, I think Ian McKellen on that occasion, probably. I cherish the worst notice I have ever had, which I got for Macbeth. I mean, you sweated your guts out, it really does take it out of you, that part, and I read the next day: 'Sir Michael Hordern reminds us of nothing so much as an Armenian carpet seller who would not have been allowed in to the back portcullis of Dunsinane.'!! That really takes it out of you.

Who wrote that?

Alan Brien. Which is a pity really, as it is not dramatic criticism. And on my night, I wasn't too bad I think, sometimes.

You came to work at the new National Theatre. How long have you spent there, on and off?

Mostly off. Well I had been at the Old Vic, you see, when the Vic first became the National Theatre, Olivier in charge. I'd been there in Tom Stoppard's *Jumpers* and when they packed up at the Vic and went down the road to the South Bank, they revived *Jumpers* and I went there then. Then they produced it again, three or four years later, and Peter Hall asked me to go back and do it again. So I did three revivals of *Jumpers*.

I remember seeing you in The Rivals *there within the last three or four years. How did you find working in that building?*

A bit soulless. I served in aircraft carriers during the war, 'Illustrious' was my ship, and the National reminds me very much of an aircraft carrier, only built with cement and anchored by the Thames. I played in two theatres – *Jumpers* in the Lyttelton, and *The Rivals* in the Olivier.

How did you find acting in the Olivier?

I liked it. I didn't find it difficult. I found it much easier than the Lyttelton. The Lyttelton is such a very odd shape: so wide, no centre aisle, the audience is a great big block. I found it easier at the Olivier.

Which theatre you have worked in gives you the fondest memories?

Hmm. Well, I suppose the Old Vic. And the Haymarket will probably come up.

ACTORS SPEAKING

Yes, the Haymarket is delightful, isn't it?

But the Old Vic was home from home.

Have you played theatres like Hampstead or the Royal Court?

The Royal Court, yes. I did a play called *Stripworld* not so very long ago.

What about the Memorial Theatre in Stratford?

Not awfully easy to play in. Easier now than it was the first time I played there; they've brought the theatre round the sides, it's more intimate than it was. But it was all so exciting to me just playing there.

What do you think of the studio theatres, like the Cottesloe?

Splendid. I've seen plays at the Cottesloe, and done a sort of Platform thing there on Izaak Walton. Yes, I have a lot of time for the fringe theatres; there was no such thing when I was an up-and-coming actor. The Arts was about the only sort of equivalent.

Going back to the Arts Theatre under Alec Clunes: what sort of policy did he have?

I don't think he had any great policy apart from enthusiasm and catholic taste. *Saints Day*, the extraordinary play that I did there, was the result of a competition, for instance. I've forgotten how many thousand entries they had, and one of the prizes was a production of the play at the Arts Theatre. The one that won first prize was this John Whiting play, *Saints Day*. But I don't think he had a definite policy, not what they are pleased to call a house style, which seems to me a very dangerous thing altogether.

I want to ask you about the influence of repertory theatres during the forties and fifties. Was Birmingham Rep formidable at that point?

Yes, I think Birmingham was formidable and Liverpool. Of course, they weren't weekly rep, they were very superior – two or three weeks. It was a gentleman's life. They are still going, are they not?

They are. They're slightly different now: rehearse for four weeks, play for six weeks, and you are engaged for just the one play.

Oh yes, they no longer have repertory companies. We absolutely lived together. We ate together, we slept together! They were real communities.

And supported by the local community too?

Absolutely. Of course there was no transport in those days, you couldn't get about. If people wanted to go to the theatre, they had to go to their nearest theatre. Now they get into their cars and go for hundreds of miles.

Is there any particular part you would still like to play?

No. I've never had any ambitions to play any particular part, never. People have always said, as I'm sure they do to every actor, 'Surely you'd love to play so-and-so?' And I have never had an ambition to play anything. People would say, 'Surely you'd love to play King Lear?' I said, if anyone was stupid enough to want me for the part I'd have a go. Which they did, and I did have a go. The only part that I have ever opted to play was Macbeth at the Old Vic. Douglas Seale, who was running that season, said, 'We'd like you to come back for a season and offer you a plum. Is there any plum you would particularly like to pick?' So I said, 'Yes, I'd like to have a go at Macbeth,' and I turned out to be an Armenian carpetseller!

ATHENE SEYLER

Were you influenced by a particular teacher, director or colleague at an early stage in your career?

Well, I went to the RADA where one had an assortment of different teachers and I wouldn't say I picked up one or another of them. They were all pretty marvellous, I thought.

Were you taught actual voice production?

Yes, voice production, but speaking no. I should think I was so bad at it that they didn't bother with me.

Why?

Oh well because it's not, as you notice, my particular forte.

But you played many classical roles in your career, didn't you?

Yes, but they were nearly all 18th-century things I've done. I've only played two Shakespearean parts.

You played Titania once upon a time…

That's right. I'd forgotten that. The only thing I did nicely in that was to go to sleep.

What other colleagues have influenced you?

Oh, you see they all belong to a period so long ago. Lena Ashwell [1872–1957], the first person who engaged me for a part, she was the person that I admired and looked up to.

When you were a very young woman did you go to the theatre a lot?

No, I couldn't afford it. I was very poor.

So you didn't see people on whom you modelled yourself?

No.

How did you know about the RADA, or the ADA as it was?

I persuaded my mother (because my father had gone by that time) that I was going on the stage. She wanted me to be a musician and play the piano, but I was shocking, I never was able to do anything at it. I said I must go into the theatre, that's what I want to do. You see I played all the leading parts at school, you know. How silly this sounds, but I had made quite a little thing for myself and my school. I said, I must go up and see if I can get an interview at the ADA. They were seeing a few people, and I was the last on the list. I remember so well, I had a light coat, the colour of your trousers, short sleeves and black gloves, which I thought was very smart. I was put in a room to wait to be called in to the judges. They were Lena Ashwell, who ran the Kingsway Theatre and was one of only three women who had ever been in commercial management, Squire Bancroft [1841–1926], and Charles Hawtrey [1858–1923]. Anyway, as I waited, I thought, 'Now shall I take off my gloves, or shall I perhaps do it in my gloves?' I thought, 'I'll take them off.' I managed to get one off when I was called in, so I was like a sort of zebra. When I'd finished my little bit, they said, 'Who taught you that?' So I said that nobody taught it, I just learnt it. 'Oh, and nobody has shown you what to do?' 'No,' I said. So they said, 'Right, now you can have a scholarship.'

Can you remember what the piece was?

Yes, it's the bit where Rosalind ticks off the shepherd for following her, in *As You Like It*. While I was at the ADA I won every prize. I must say I had a very comfortable time there.

Didn't you become the first President of RADA who had been one of its students?

Yes. And I don't think they've had any since as far as I know.

Do you think there has been a change in the way people speak in the theatre since you were a young girl?

Athene Seyler in John van Druten's *Bell, Book and Candle*, Phoenix Theatre, 1954
(Mander & Mitchenson Theatre Collection)

Oh yes, I think there must be, because modern speech is awfully slipshod.

What do you think good speaking is? What do you think an actor is doing when he is speaking well?

Not listening to his own voice, which some of them do. I think the whole point really is to get the truth of what they're saying over; people who listen to their own voices have probably lost the sense and the theme of what they're saying.

Are there any actors you particularly admire or who you think speak well?

Edith Evans, she was a beautiful speaker. And darling Henry Ainley [1879–1945], he had a lovely voice and spoke beautifully. But people like Mrs Patrick Campbell [1865–1940], who had a rather plummy voice, that sort of thing I think is bad speaking, I hated it. She never could speak quite plainly. Nowadays I don't see enough theatre to judge, and I don't hear well when I do. I haven't seen any very exciting acting on television lately, though I'm not at all sure that's a fair judgement. But you can still distinguish between thrilling acting and what just makes you think, 'Hmm, how funny that you want to act.' I've always felt that I like to tell people something, that's why I like acting. That's why I didn't enjoy filming ever, really, because I like a live audience.

Do you miss it?

Not now, dear, no, not as a great-grandmother. No, not really... One grandson is a television director, another's going into the army – how extraordinary – another's hoping to go into the church. We've rather thrown the theatre over in my family. Of course now you have to belong to a trade union. I hate trades unions. I used to always arrange my own salary with the management. If Binkie Beaumont was engaging me for a part at the Haymarket, he would say, 'Now what about money darling, what is it you want?' And I would say, 'Well, I don't know, what did you pay me last time?' And he said, 'Athene, you're the only person I know who doesn't argue about money,' and he put £10 a week on my salary at once.

Did you work at the Old Vic?

I knew Lilian Baylis before she took over the Old Vic. I knew her and her aunt when it was a music hall. I came back from Australia and played the Nurse in *Romeo and Juliet* there. Claire Bloom was my Juliet.

Would you approach the speaking in the same way for a classical part or a modern part?

Exactly the same way. I think the only thing that is necessary for every branch of acting is truth. If you're thinking of the truth of what you're doing, you walk right and you think right, and then you speak well.

How do you discover that truth?

Well, you dig about in the play you're doing and find it – the truth of a scene or the truth of a relationship. So long as that is the first thing in your head, then you'll probably speak the right way, you see. It will tell you that here you must hurry, and there pause, because you're thinking truthfully about it. That's my only rule. I don't think you can lay down rules otherwise, do you?

If an actor is speaking badly, what is he doing?

Oh, sloppy speech I hate…

What do you mean by sloppy speech?

Not using the consonants properly, and bad sounds for vowels. Of course you've got to have a beautiful voice to start with. I think that's essential. That's why I never could speak verse because I wasn't given a beautiful voice like Edith. Edith Evans had a lovely voice, really beautiful.

You've twice expressed your limitations about your own voice, but it's very expressive and mobile, isn't it?

It's a useful comedy voice, that I do know, but it's no good for speaking poetry or Shakespeare. It's not got a nice sound.

So you never expected to play the romantic parts?

Oh no.

But you did play Hermia and Rosalind.

Yes, Rosalind I adored. I played her twice for different companies. First with Nigel Playfair at Hammersmith. There's a lot of prose in Rosalind. I think there must be a difference in one's attitude: in verse you're really listening to the way it's made; in prose you're only thinking about the meaning of it. But I've never been able to speak verse really. I don't think I've ever tried much.

We have lots of questions about the techniques of verse. In verse, does end-stopping matter? Do you know what end-stopping is?

Haven't a clue, dear.

You never came across any of these terms – end-stopping, caesura, feminine endings, rhyming couplets – you must have come across rhyming couplets.

Yes, I suppose I have… It all depends on if I'm enjoying it, you see if I can enjoy it, then I shall know how to speak it.

Do you have anything to say about audibility?

(*Laughs.*) It must be, it simply must.

Was it always? When you were a younger woman, was the actor's stock-in-trade that he could be heard in whatever theatre he played?

Yes. Of course some theatres are more difficult than others. I always loved Drury Lane, you know. I remember once somebody left a car in the street where I live that was blocking the way. I said, 'How disgraceful, I bet they're in the pub.' So I went to the pub and it was absolutely full, the noise was incomparable because everyone was talking. I thought to myself, Well, I've been heard at the very back of the gallery at Drury Lane, so I'll try this… 'Man with the car…!' and there was dead silence in a moment! If you're a comedy actress, which obviously I'm nothing else but, you're aware that if you're not audible, you lose your laughs.

Is there a great difference between comedy acting and tragic?

Oh yes, there's a great difference. Tragic acting is so very inside, isn't it? Comedy acting is entirely, from my point of view, outside. Tragic acting is yourself enduring something. Comedy acting is telling somebody else about it. Now that to me is the difference.

But I suppose the truth still has to be found?

Oh yes, that's obvious. That's why I think modern acting is good. I'm sure people are much more concerned with what they're doing properly than with what other people are thinking about them. At least, that's how it strikes me.

You played at the Haymarket quite a lot, didn't you?

Eight times. I adored it, it's my theatre. I played in every theatre in London except the Adelphi, and I think my favourite is the Haymarket. It's a beautiful theatre, with a lovely tradition, and it has a ghost. He knocks on the principal dressing room door occasionally, but doesn't come in. He just knocks and goes away. But the ghost I saw absolutely was at the old Royalty theatre, which now they've pulled down. It was in Soho, a nice little old theatre but awfully slummy at the back, so people always used the front of house to come in, then you went across the stage and up to your dressing room. One day the stage manager said, 'There's been an old woman up in that box.' We stared, but the box was quite empty, and she said, 'But I distinctly saw an old lady there.' When I was going out through the front of house that night, I looked into the empty theatre and there, in the middle of the stalls, was an old lady. I said to the commissionaire, 'You know the audience hasn't all gone, don't you?' He went back in, and said, 'Of course they've gone, who did you think you saw?' I said, 'There was an old lady there.' He said, 'Oh yes, that's the ghost.'

Did you find yourself helped by directors at any stage in your life?

Oh dear, I can remember the opposite... Tony Guthrie, directing me in the great Russian play, *The Cherry Orchard*. There's a scene where she's standing by the window looking out, 'My orchard, my cherry orchard', and I was enjoying it immensely. Suddenly his voice from the back of the theatre: 'Look, darling, we don't want any Athene Seyler tricks in this scene.' Oh my goodness, what it did to me, because of course I had no idea what he meant. If you've got any tricks, you don't know them or you wouldn't be doing them. For days I couldn't play the bothering part at all. Charles Laughton was in it with me. He wasn't there for the first rehearsals because he hadn't come back from America or somewhere. There was a scene in which, rehearsing with the understudy, I wept. When Charles came and played the scene with me, he began to cry too, and so I had to stop crying. We couldn't both weep, it would be idiotic.

Did you not take very much notice of directors during your career?

Not very much, I must say. I remember Charles Hawtrey saying to an actor, 'I want you to sit on the sofa here. No, not like that. Just sit. Don't you see what I mean?' And then he lowered himself down on that sofa in such a marvellous way that it was terribly funny, and of course the poor actor couldn't do it at all.

How long would you have rehearsed a play at that time?

Oh, three weeks or so. And if you were a quick study, you learnt it at the first reading practically. I actually was a very quick study.

When you were a young woman was there such a thing as a director?
They were called producers, weren't they?

In those days the author used to read his play to the assembled company. One of them had such a frightful cockney accent it was torture listening. He was spoiling his own play for us to listen to. And then, when he'd finished, we'd start rehearsals. The first producer I had said, 'Now Miss Seyler, this is your scene. Where would you like to play it?' I'm not sure it was an awfully good idea because you couldn't tell where you wanted to be, except damn well down front and centre.

Did you ever act in any of Shaw's plays? He was a great one for
reading his plays, wasn't he?

Yes, I played Proserpine in *Candida*. He was a great bore and had to be turned out of the theatre at rehearsals. He would ask for things and call out and do this, that and the other, and the producer wouldn't have it. We had a little difference of opinion about Proserpine. I had to get up from typing and make an exit after a scene. It was a long way round from downstage left, right up to the back. It was to be funny, you see, and so Shaw shouted from the back, 'Look here, fall over the mat there, we want a laugh.' I thought the hell with that, and how I got my laugh was to make an enormous circle round all of them very fast without falling over the mat, and that always got a huge laugh.

When did that fashion of the author reading his play finish?

Oh, quite soon after I went on the stage. I only remember that happening twice. I don't think it will ever happen again. In my early days, you didn't know what part the manager wanted you for. He would engage you, then you went to the first rehearsal and were given sides. Did you know we called them sides? It was just sheets printed with your part and just three words for a cue with little dots. People would say, 'How many sides have you got?' which meant how big was your part. And that was the first one knew about the play or one's part or anything else.

ROBERT STEPHENS

*Were you influenced by a particular teacher, director or colleague at
an early stage in your career?*

The greatest influence was a man called Anthony Thomas. He ran an arts
centre in Cranbrook, Kent, and a travelling theatre which toured to youth
clubs. I did two tours, ten weeks each, as a boy actor, and he said I think
maybe you should go on the stage. He got me an audition with Esmé
Church [1873–1972], who was a great visionary about theatre. Before the
war, she ran the Old Vic School and helped people like Ralph Richardson,
Laurence Olivier, Alec Guinness. She was also a director and directed
Edith Evans in her famous production of *As You Like It* when she played
Rosalind. During the war the Old Vic moved their operation to Buxton,
and she saw there was an enormous amount of talent in the north. So after
the war she opened the Northern Theatre School which ran successfully
for about seven years. From my audition I got a free scholarship to the
drama school. I had a very heavy Bristolian accent which of course I
thought I must get rid of.

*What was it particularly that Esmé Church conveyed to you about
speaking?*

Well, that acting is extremely difficult and therefore you have to work
very hard at it because your body is simply a machine which you must be
in control of all the time – in speaking and in moving and in everything to
do with it. A piece of equipment. The more finely tuned it is, the better
actor you will be and the more flexible in your concept of different parts
and ways of playing them.

Were there particular exercises she set you, or things she said?

Robert Stephens as Molière's Tartuffe (translated by Richard Wilbur), with Kenneth Mackintosh, National Theatre at the Old Vic, 1967 (NT Archive, Photo Angus McBean)

She had a movement teacher called Rudolf Laban, who was the first man to notate modern dance steps. He had a big studio in Manchester and would come every Thursday. He said, 'All the exercises I give you are for dancers, not for actors, but just do them and you can reduce it.'

Which directors you have worked with have been influential?

Somebody asked me what it was like being directed by Noël Coward. I said, 'I simply can't tell you,' because you never realise for one second that you're being directed. He would sometimes say, 'A bit common, a bit common.' He just nursed it through. He insisted you knew every line at the first rehearsal. I said, 'Why do you insist on that?' He said, 'I will tell you why. Because learning lines is very easy. Acting is very difficult. So get rid of the book. My plays are written in short lines. It's not like playing Coriolanus where you have to pick your way through.' He said that in playing comedy, what you have to do is hold the audience like a thoroughbred horse and not let them run away with you. In the first act, keep a tight rein on them and cut through every laugh. Second act, let them go a little bit but not too much. Third act, let them go. He said the interesting thing about laughter is that too much can tire them out, so don't let them get tired in the first act, because you have to hit a target. The target is the final curtain.

What about John Dexter?

John is a fine director, but he's not a good actors' director. When we did *Royal Hunt of the Sun* he thought he had made me a star, which was rubbish. I don't think I got one note from him about that part. I made it all up myself, by going to the gymnasium, by listening to Mexican music and finding out all about it. But as a director of spectacle he is very good. He's certainly good at saying, 'Do it faster,' or, 'Speak louder.'

Ingmar Bergman is the best director I ever worked with. He judges your performance in every way to the millimetre. And he's the most delightful person – charming, sweet, funny – and you would think of him as rather heavy and melancholic. Not at all. Very light-hearted. I think all the actors in *Hedda Gabler* felt absolutely safe and secure in his production because he directed it half like a theatre play and half like a film. His lighting plot was like a film, terribly complicated, because he would pull people in and out of focus by a very subtle change. The audience couldn't see it; it was imperceptible to the human eye. It meant that if he told you to sit like so, you had to play the scene like that – move and you'll not be lit properly. But that's all right, it's just another way of acting. It certainly puts a discipline on you.

Tyrone Guthrie was another great director. He said there are a lot of things that opera singers can learn from actors, and there are things that actors can learn from opera. One thing you can learn, which is important in Shakespeare, is that you must be able to say ten lines on one breath without stopping. He said what you can use is the snatched breath, which they use in opera. You just take a little bit to top up.

What do you think is meant by good speaking? If an actor is speaking well, what is he doing?

It's a very difficult thing to learn, but in the end you can do it. You have to use diaphragmatic control. You have to lift the ribcage and keep it lifted, which means you spread all the intercostal muscles and fill yourself with as much air as you can get. Take the breath when the other person is speaking, two lines before he finishes his speech, so you are ready to carry on, bang, bang bang. If you are running out, just lift it again. It's entirely a technical exercise and it took me a long time to learn how to do it. Laurence Olivier's back was incredibly broad, because he played so much Shakespeare. The ribcage expands. I met a very famous opera star, a woman called Elena Suliotis. She came to the place where I was living and I had a gramophone record of her famous performance in *Nabucco*. I said, 'Can I play a bit?' So I put it on, and she sang too, and the walls shook with the power of her voice. I said, 'May I feel your ribcage?'; 'What for?' I said, 'Well I'm an actor and I'd like to feel how far it goes out.' She said, 'You don't sing from there. The legs support the voice.' Different techniques.

So the technique for you…?

As much as you can, be endlessly relaxed. Of course one is in some kind of tension when you go on a stage. Of course you are. I was in the wings with Edith Evans, while we were doing *Hay Fever*, and she said, 'Are you nervous?' I said, 'Well, yes.' She said, 'That's right. The moment you aren't nervous, you won't be any good.'

If an actor is speaking badly, what is he doing?

He is not paying sufficient attention to the text. You have to examine it, think it through, feel it through. Bill Gaskill used improvisation a lot. On *The Recruiting Officer* he improvised for two weeks with no text. You would read the scene and then do it in your own words, just to see what you missed out. He said it seemed to him that in lots of Shakespeare and classical plays, the actors don't know what they are talking about, so they say, 'I'll just speak it fast and it'll be all right.' He said, if you know the thoughts in a play, you'll never dry. You might say something different, but at least it will carry on. If you don't know the thoughts and you dry, you're dead because you simply have no idea what you're talking about. I think you should never treat a long speech as a long speech, because as we talk we change our minds, get reminded of something else. If you find thoughts, you can fragment it. That colours it for the audience and sounds natural. I was taught to hold a mirror up to nature; that's what you have to do.

Do you think end-stopping matters?

I think they should republish Shakespeare's plays so that they look like ordinary plays – run it all the way through, and ignore all the punctuation. Because actors fall into the trap of stopping at line endings. I think with all lines you must shoot to the end, as it were, taking a dart and shooting at a bullseye. You have to fill an enormous area, a thousand people, their clothes and the covered seats all absorb sound. The rising inflection is important always.

Which other colleagues do you admire?

One of the best actors I've worked with of my contemporaries is Colin Blakely [1930–87]. I did lots of plays with him, and what Colin has is flexibility, but you also trust him. I don't think that any two performances of *The Royal Hunt of the Sun* were exactly the same. You have to trust the other actor; it's like playing good tennis or doing good boxing, I suppose, if you trust the person you are working with. It didn't matter what he did because it was always controlled.

What about people like Olivier, with whom you've worked a lot?

Well the marvellous thing about when Laurence ran the National Theatre company was that, because we only had one theatre, all the actors saw him all the time, in the canteen, in the corridor, on the stage, so you knew who was the top of the pyramid. Being a very clever fellow, he made it his business to know everybody's name. So if a new actor joined the company he would say, 'What's that boy's name?'; 'It's Peter.' So Laurence would go to him and say, 'Peter, how very nice it is to have you in our company, I do hope you will enjoy yourself.'

But as an actor, he had a rather idiosyncratic way of speaking classical text, didn't he?

Well, you like it or you don't. For his Othello, he made himself look frightfully attractive with his make-up. He must have tried twenty different variations. It originally took him five hours to put the make-up on; he must have gone through twenty thousand wig fittings to get the wig right. I mean, the sheer pyrotechnics of his acting were quite dazzling: to see someone who was at every single moment during his performance totally in control of what he was doing. He had thought that part through completely. I was on a train with him once, coming from Brighton. He said, 'Do you know what I do every day, coming up and down to Brighton? I've learned the whole of my part as Othello.' That was exactly seven months before the first reading of the play. I said to Frank Finlay who was playing the Iago, and who is a very fine actor, but had never played Shakespeare before, 'Do yourself a favour. Laurence knows all of it, he's possibly the greatest actor in the world, and he's played more Shakespeare than you've had hot dinners. So learn it.' Frank said, 'Well, I don't know that I should until I know what it's going to be like.' I said, 'Just learn it.' Frank chose not to. Consequently, Laurence danced him out of the exit door.

I've only seen the film…

The film's quite different. Frank in fact was better in the film. Afterwards, while we were rehearsing *Three Sisters*, Laurence said to me, 'You're playing a colonel in the Russian army, but you keep using your hands all the time. Soldiers are used to dealing with cannons and things; their hands are heavy.' He said, 'When I did the film of *Othello*, the director didn't tell me to stop using my hands. All you see is me rolling my eyes around and being theatrical. If he had just said, "Cut all the gestures," it would have been all right. But nobody told me, so now I'm telling you. Don't use your hands to act unless you're playing Goldoni.'

Who among your younger contemporaries do you think speaks well?

Ian McKellen speaks very well. Still a slight touch of a northern accent, but it doesn't matter. I think Alan Howard speaks very well. Also Ian Holm. There are lots of them – Ronald Pickup, Anthony Hopkins.

Do you think it's impossible to speak well in a regional accent?

You can speak all right, but you have so many twisted vowel sounds.

Has there been a change in speaking in the theatre in your lifetime?

I think it changed when the English Stage Company at the Royal Court opened with *Look Back in Anger* and all those people were encouraged to retain their provincial accents. All those actors (and this is no criticism) like Albert Finney, Peter O'Toole, Joan Plowright, Alan Bates, Tom Courtenay, have never really lost that flat sound which can be slightly boring, I think, because it has no colour. That's the way they speak when they're at home with their mothers and fathers, but it's not quite the way you speak on stage. Of course it doesn't matter, but to me it is not believable to have Hamlet or Macbeth speaking like a Cockney or a Mancunian because the audience relate to the kings and queens we have, who certainly don't speak as though they came from Scunthorpe.

But I don't think you can speak Shakespeare properly with vowels as narrow as some of the royal family.

No, that's true. But I do think you need to be able to speak standard English.

Would you approach the discipline of speaking a classical and a modern role in the same way?

Absolutely. If you can speak classical text, which is difficult because it's not the way in which we speak nowadays, then you can speak any text at all. It teaches you the discipline of speaking and making sense out of what is not the normal pattern of speech.

How do you reconcile the actor's personal need for expressiveness
with the demands of the text?

Well you can't get away from what's written on the page. You may think,
I would have said that differently, but you are stuck with what the person
wrote. You've just got to make it your own. With those things, a director
can help you. But some directors can't quite make themselves clear about
what they want. I remember Peter Wood saying to Michael Redgrave, 'A
little less Beethoven. A little more Bach.' Redgrave said, 'What exactly
do you mean by that? I don't understand what you mean.' I think in all
directing and acting of plays the venture is entirely co-operative. The great
thing to remember as a director is that you're on the top of a pyramid, and
you're responsible for all the stones underneath, whether it be the stage
manager, the wig lady, whatever. You have to control the whole thing and
keep everybody happy. Many directors are frightful bullies. If you start
bullying some actor, you shouldn't have cast him. If you make an actor
nervous by telling them they're no good, they can't do it. Then you waltz
off on the first night with your two and a half per cent of the gross, and the
actor is left for the rest of the run thinking they are no good.

Who in your experience could be imitated without being a bad
influence as an actor?

I think what you have to do, if you see somebody do something on the
stage which is marvellous, is sort of put it in your back pocket. It's no
good trying to imitate Laurence Olivier, although people do of course.
What you can do is take his techniques and reinterpret them through
yourself. He told me that when he was a young actor he was influenced
by three actors: Ronald Colman [1891–1958] – he even grew a little thin
moustache like Ronald Colman; Alfred Lunt [1892–1977] who he said
taught him how to act with his back to the audience; and John Barrymore
[1882–1942]. Olivier saw Barrymore playing Hamlet when he came over
before the war. He said he pinched being very athletic from him. He just
picked those tricks up and kept them in a pocket. He said that all actors
are magpies, they steal from each other.

Madoline Thomas as the Nurse in Chekhov's *Uncle Vanya* (version by Pam Gems), with Patti Love,
National Theatre in the Lyttelton, 1982 (NT Archive, Photo Laurence Burns)

MADOLINE THOMAS

*Were you influenced by a particular teacher, director or colleague at
an early stage in your career?*

Yes, yes, yes. Very, very influenced. My mother was one of eighteen
children. Her poor mother lived with eighteen kids running around. This
was in Abergavenny. One of the girls had the talent, and in the end she
was allowed to go. Her name was Barbara Gott and she was a beautiful
actress. She was the most beautiful woman I think I've ever seen. When
I was three and a half I told my mother I'm going to be an actress, and
my mother put on her hat and coat and went down to the church and
prayed for me. Trade you see. Oh terrible! And then another aunt says,
'I'll smuggle you up to London and you shall visit Auntie Gott and see her
act.' I was twelve or thirteen by this time. She smuggled me up and Auntie
Gott put us up in her little flat. I said, 'But we'll never get inside, it's like
a doll's house.' We lived in a great big house, you see. Anyway, I thought it
was heaven. Do you know a play called *Three Sisters*? She was in that. Oh
she was marvellous, and to this day I could tell you almost every move that
she made. My aunt said that I never murmured, hardly breathed all the
way home. Somehow I was guided not ever to say anything to my mother
about it. I was sorry for my mother, you see, terribly sorry. She had no joy
– couldn't have without the stage.

Well, years later Peter Hall rang me up and said, 'Darling, do you
know a play called *Three Sisters*? Would you like to play in it?' And it was
just as if I'd had twelve months' rehearsal. I learnt the words in about a
night; they were all here, packed up in my brain. And Peter said, 'It's the
best thing you've ever done.' Well of course it was because it was Auntie
Gott, it wasn't me at all.

When my mother saw me acting she would say, 'Well, I don't admire
your taste. What I'd like to see would be you behind the frying pan, feeding

people, making them happy because of food. I don't want all these words.'
You see she didn't believe in it at all. I never remember her saying, 'Let's
go to the theatre.' A concert party came to Abergavenny on a three-night
stand, and I thought they were dreadful, they oughtn't to be allowed the
space. They came to see the show I was in and said 'Would you like to join
us?' I thought, 'Join you? I wouldn't be seen dead with you.' But then it
suddenly dawned on me that if I did I would get away from home. So I did
and we toured and went to the most horrible dates. Oh they were awful.
I thought if Mum saw this I wouldn't have a chance, but it gave me a start
because I then met somebody of note and he said, 'You're getting out of
this, I'll get you something else.'

Who was he?

I can't remember who it was now. I don't remember names well. I don't
know *your* names and I never shall! I have, on one occasion, forgotten my
own.

What is it they are they trying to do with this study?

*Peter [Gill] thinks that people don't speak as well now as they used
to. He's trying to find out why it is that someone like you speaks so
well, how you learnt to do it, and perhaps pass that information on.
Who else have you been influenced by?*

There are so many actresses and actors that have more than satisfied me.
Peggy Ashcroft, now, I worked with her a lot at the RSC. We did a whole
year of all the Histories and it was very heavy. Ooh my God it was heavy.
But I don't like the comedies, you see. I can't smile at Mr Shakespeare
when he's trying to be funny, I think he's a bore. But his tragedies, oh my
God, they eat your heart out. Well now, Peggy and I between us – I'm not
meaning to say I'm on the same stepladder as Peggy, no no no – but we
were always put to play the Queens you see. I was always the blooming
old Queen. Oh Peggy was marvellous, I have never seen such work – with
her hands and her feet and her altogether – as that girl got into it. I used
to ask permission to go down early for my entrance to watch Peggy and
learn, learn. I'm still like that. I want to learn something all the time. I'm
so greedy. I used to go down and stand in the wings and watch this girl
enter. No one makes an entrance like Peggy. The whole theatre sitting

up, you can almost hear the noise of them sitting up. She had to do a very long, low curtsy, right down so her little bottom was on the floor. I thought, 'She'll go arse over tip, when she gets up her legs will be stiff.' So I was biting my nails in the wings, but not a rustle. She had a lot of gown, which she managed so beautifully. I should have been turning somersaults of course.

Did you admire her speaking?

Oh, oh beautiful. I mean, right up from the tummy, up up up, all the time.

Did anyone teach you about speaking when you were first in the theatre?

No, no. I think it was common sense, and I've got a lot to be thankful for. I had a father and a mother who were the most beautifully spoken people. They were aristocrats, for want of a better word. You're young both of you, but please please find out what good things you've got in life – parents, friends, anybody – and value them beyond keeping, because I've got nothing to do now but think. I think back and think dear God you've been good to me.

What do you think is meant by speaking well?

Well you've got a tummy and you've got lungs. You must have good breathing before you can do anything at all. And not only good breathing but you must know how to spend your breathing. It's like your weekly housekeeping money. You can't spend it all on Monday night. It's got to last until Saturday. So you must have complete control of your lungs, and that I think is the most difficult part. When I was young, the master that I had, ooh, he was a Tartar. He used to put heavy great boxes of stuff on your stomach, and you had to rise enough to knock them off. It was very hard training but by jingo I can last now.

Where was this?

In Bristol. An aunt and uncle who were very wealthy said, 'There's nothing for her in Abergavenny, let her come to us and live in Bristol.' So I lived with them for years as their child, and every day I went to this engagement room where you could have piano lessons, singing lessons, speaking lessons. I learnt right from the word A and finally got to Z. My father came to me and said, 'You want the stage?' I said, 'Yes, I don't want anything else.' 'Right,' he said, 'I'm going to ask you to do the impossible. You've got to have a letter after your name. You've got to take a degree in harmony, singing or conducting, so that if you're a bloody awful actress you can sing to them, charm them. The cheapest course is two years, and I can't afford to keep you two years, so you've got to get two degrees in one year. You'd better start tonight.' And I did. I knew a lot about music, but nothing like what was wanted. But I got them, those two degrees. How, I do not know.

Where did you study?

I did all the learning from two masters in Bristol. One was very well known, a Mr Blanchard. He taught me organ and piano. The other was Herr Sondeman, a German gentleman. He was a marvellous singing tutor. He used to go all over the country giving lectures on good breathing. Consumption had come to the foreground in those days, and he reckoned this was because we didn't know how to breathe. These two worked very hard on me and I got a medal for something. It was only a bit of brass; I gave it to my youngest great grandchild.

Do you think there has been a change in speaking in the theatre?

Oh yes. A big change. I remember saying to a young girl I was working with, 'Put your tongue out.' She said, 'Oh I mustn't do that, it's rude.' Anyway, she put it out, and I said, 'Now you see that vessel is one of the most important which has been given to you, and you talk as if someone had just given you a pound of sour plums. You can talk with your tongue. And what about your teeth? Why do you try to talk over the top of your teeth? The teeth are there to keep your tongue in its place.' Now you see there are schools that teach nothing else but your whole body.

Do you think actors are taught differently now?

Oh yes. They haven't got the affectation. It's disappearing from this generation. You've got that girl Peggy [Ashcroft] to thank for that. That girl never mouths the words. You should never do that. You want your mouth, your lips, your teeth, your tongue, your glottis – everything you've got must work. If you're going to be lazy then you won't be heard.

With Shakespeare, do you apply different rules to prose and verse?

I find Shakespeare's tragedies very absorbing and loved to work in them. But I do think he is used far more than he need be. I think there are other writers who are just as good. Another thing is that they're always used as a punishment. I was always sent upstairs to my bedroom and told to learn a scene off by heart. I think that goes on quite a lot you know.

Do you approach learning a classical play as you would a modern one?

Yes. It's a pitfall that people think, 'I'm speaking Shakespeare; I've got to speak it *so*.' No, no. He was a human man altogether. He lived a long time ago, and perhaps some words even had a quite different meaning then, but the gist of the matter is still there. I don't think anything need be specialised or dressed up. The beauty of it is to enjoy it and to understand it.

We were going to ask about the way you learned to speak verse. Did you learn rules about speaking verse?

Yes, up to a point, but never to the point of altering the verse. You mustn't have in your mind the thought that this line is divided into two ends. If it's said naturally, it's all right. But you hear people getting a sing-song tone because it's verse. The thing to do, I find, is to practise it as one big sentence, and then divide it up.

Which other younger actors have you admired?

Oh so many. There's one young girl – Cherie Lunghi. Now I consider her really something. She was with me in *Uncle Vanya* at the National, playing the lead. I liked her work in that very much indeed.

Did you find the Olivier Theatre, where you did Tales from the Vienna Woods, *difficult to play?*

To get your voice over? No, there's no difficulty at all. There are some people who find it difficult because they just jolly well don't know how to speak. All right, take your breath, open your mouth and speak. It isn't a matter of how loud your voice is, never let anyone tell you that. It doesn't matter if you've only got a small voice so long as you say the words very very distinctly, and remember that they're not only going to the front row. Peter Hall (and you can ask him to verify this) came in to one rehearsal and reprimanded us that we could not be heard. I thought, 'Not heard?' Couldn't understand this. And then he said, 'I don't like doing this, but I must say I don't think there is one theatre or hall in London that Madoline couldn't fill.' It was the greatest compliment I've ever had. He said to me, 'How do you do it?' I said, 'By using all I've got: my lips, my teeth, my chest, my tummy, everything.' You can't stand up on a stage and look beautiful and all that and not move. You can't. Think first of what you're going to say and how you're going to say it, and how far you're going to send it.

MARGARET TYZACK

When did you first act in Shakespeare?

When I first came to Shakespeare, when I went to the RSC, I'd been doing a lot of television. It wasn't really deliberate, but my telly life had gone ahead of my theatre life a bit, and I had spent a lot of time doing the sort of scripts where you eliminated the language you were given because it was so bad. You twisted it, glossed it up, tarted it up, manipulated it. But when you actually came to something like Shakespeare, that you could use on the line, boom, it was a great shock to the system. Shakespeare is a big garment, and if you're not really ready for it, it's like putting on an overcoat that's much too big for you and you get swamped by it.

It's interesting what you were saying earlier about having to make an
effort with fairly indifferent television scripts, to put something into
them textually, and then going to Shakespeare. How do you feel after
a length of time doing Shakespeare?

I feel enriched. I don't feel, Gosh, I can't do a telly any more, but it doesn't negate the things you've learnt, they don't have to be thrown away again, not by a long shot. Well, things like size do, obviously. If I did a television the way I'm playing the part I'm currently playing on stage, it would just swamp it. When it's Shakespeare, I suppose I'm a little bit elitist, and pay him rather more regard than perhaps I do with some other author.

Were you influenced by a particular teacher, director or colleague at
an early stage in your career?

I was influenced by a teacher called Elizabeth Pursey who taught me in my last year at the Convent. She made me want to come into the theatre, but then I didn't meet her again until years later, and now she is my teacher when I want help, and she is quite remarkable. The person I first worked with in rep was called Chloe Gibson. For her time she had a great simplicity. The pressure was dreadful, of doing a play a week, but we used to do a fortnight of half days, so that made it a little bit better. She would say, 'Never do something until you feel with every fibre of your being that it is the only way you could express what you want to.' That ties in with something I had written down when I did *All's Well* – 'The actor must earn the right to speak the lines.' The lines are the end process, and in every scene, every speech, you must ask yourself exactly what the character is seeking to achieve and, having singled out an objective, narrow it down by patient experiment until it becomes so specific that the lines written are the only possible means of expressing it. Does that make sense? It's so obvious really, and it sounds so simplistic, but when you go away from those truths, that's when you can get into trouble. You can get seduced into all sorts of odd things, then you come back to your dressing room and you've written that down, and you think, 'Uh-huh.' Another one I had is 'Not how you say it but why you say it', which can be a great guiding light, I think.

What younger colleagues do you admire or have you been influenced by?

Well one of the younger ones is Helen Mirren. I think Helen speaks very well. When I was very very young, and the modern influences were coming across the Atlantic, I couldn't understand why Dame Peggy's generation of actor was as venerated as it was. I can now. With Dame Peggy it's something to do with her integrity that I admire. Her compassion, too. I think there's something in the woman herself that I admire.

If an actor is speaking well, what is he doing?

If he wasn't, you'd notice it. If an actor is speaking badly, then he's being self-indulgent.

What about changes in the theatre that you've observed over your lifetime?

The development of the visual arts in my span in the theatre, which is over thirty years, is remarkable. And the devaluation of the language; the way we now all have a fuck and a shit and this that and the other. People

Margaret Tyzack as Martha in Edward Albee's *Who's Afraid of Virginia Woolf?*,
National Theatre in the Lyttelton, 1981 (NT Archive, Photo Zoë Dominic)

gain a lot more of their sounds from contemporary television, less from literature. Social values have changed. Listening instead of reading.

I think one of the problems, particularly with Shakespeare, is that all too often, actors don't listen.

Oh no, they don't listen enough. And that's a habit we're getting more and more from the Americans. Long ago, we went with the RSC to do a play called *Summerfolk* at the Brooklyn Academy. We went into a diner in Brooklyn and the people there weren't very nice to us. I don't know what was wrong but they weren't very nice. I then had a week off because they were doing another play, and I came back and they were fine. I said, 'What's happened? They seem nice at the diner now.' They said, 'Oh yes, they thought we were Germans speaking English.' They had just thought we were fair and that this funny different noise was German.

As far as listening is concerned, I think that's a great deal to do with the real you, your degree of self-absorption or not. You can talk to someone who will tell you about the finer points of acting, and go out on stage with them and it's like Mrs Patrick Campbell on a bad day, because it is their nature, you don't leave that behind. Sometimes it works the other way. There are people who in their life give no compassion, but can act it awfully well.

Do you think verse and prose should be treated differently?

Prose is private talk, usually, in Shakespeare, it's the private thoughts. You'll never find a speech to the people done in prose. I think that's the best way of describing it: it's private and not governed by formality, really. I think that's right. And I suppose I can contradict myself. Prose does have a rhythm, but it has the rhythm of reality. Intent must overwhelm the verse, I think that's the way I would describe it. It must never become music and if intent does overwhelm it, it never will.

Are there any disciplines in the speaking of verse that you'd like to see generally applied?

Well, the word 'generally' bothers me a bit, because everything in speaking is particular. I have to remind myself about chin up, cut, and end-stopping.

End-stopping? Well, if the meaning stops there, yes. If the meaning goes on, no.

It's what you were saying before, it's the integrity of the line, playing the line for its meaning.

But when I do Shakespeare, I kid myself that very few people would shoot me down, those people who love end-stops. Very few would shoot me down because if I'm doing the line well, it will seem right. And the meaning will seem right... There's sometimes a sort of an extra little something you want to give yourself in order to carry it on. You know, you put your feet in the water and feel it, I think.

What are the things that help audibility?

Clarity of thought helps, but all the things about gauging the size of the room you are playing in, exercising your voice to make sure that it fills that auditorium, I mean, all that to me is obvious. You know, like a cooking lesson: 'Take a saucepan – that's a thing with a handle...'

Who do you think is a good speaker?

I hate to be tied down on that, because my taste changes at different times.

What, other than acting colleagues, has influenced the way you speak?

There are a million answers to that. Environment, your parents. I speak fast because I'm from a city. You realise it when you go to the country, you know, those short, clipped tones. It's Cockney really. Years ago there was a thing on the radio called *Children's Hour*, and someone called David Davis read *The Wind in the Willows*. Now I don't know how that would sound now, but I can still hear some of it, and that must have been an enormous influence on me. You'd draw the curtains, there wasn't any telly, and you'd listen to *Children's Hour*, with Uncle Mac – he embodied it – 'Goodnight children, everywhere.'

Do you think some actors consider that any technique is a restriction and an imposition upon their personal expressiveness?

Yes. I think we've got that from across the Atlantic. I was at the Royal Court with a very good actor from America, and he was very frightened of that restriction. I think it might be because we are brought up still to be an ensemble, but they are all brought up to think each one is going to be a star. I did think, as a young actor, that if you could practically eliminate self, that was the thing to do. Totally to be a vessel of what you were playing. Disguise yourself so that you were never recognised a second time. Somebody once said, 'You've got a nice voice.' So I thought, 'That's got to go.' I mean, lunacy as far as paying the rent's concerned. I didn't get that from RADA, because we didn't all come out the same. We went in knowing nothing, and we weren't taught much, so how could we all come out the same? The thing was, you always had your accent eliminated, and I think that was pretty good. It doesn't mean you can't go back to it, but it meant you could play lots of other things. So as a young actor, I just thought that was the bee's knees. Self was a dirty word. I was a bit foolish, and took it to extremes when I was in rep, but I really used to try and empty myself and take everything on board. I think it made me rather dull for quite some time.

When I started it was rather 'gentlemen and players', you know, and I certainly wasn't in the gentleman category. If you had a rather nice suit and a rather nice voice, mostly you worked pretty well. It's harder now. Young actors work much harder and you're expected to know a lot more. It helps if you're with people who are, as much as anyone can be, honest. People who tell you things because they care and want you to be good, not because they've got some little axe to grind. That's the most dangerous thing, and that's why teacher's ego should be left at home, which is asking a lot.

You've got to do your homework, narrowing it down and narrowing it down until all there is left is the tense and the word – it could be no other way with Shakespeare. Narrowing, knowing the words, it's a wonderful freedom – you fly. I alas have never done enough Shakespeare to really feel I could fly.

I think one of the unfortunate things that has happened in British theatre is that people are a bit apprehensive about speaking. Do you know what I mean?

I think that is the case, in so many ways. So many young people, because work is difficult to find, their main experience is in a very small space. Some can have worked in the theatre for eight years and never done a classic. I find when I'm with them and we get to a bigger space, they are in agony, and very happy to take aboard 'technique'. We can get away with a lot as actors, being very lazy. A pianist can't, a dancer can't, a violinist can't. We often can. I think one is more liable to fool a certain number of people at a play than people who go and hear a concert, alas. Because of all sorts of things: 'The Emperor's New Clothes', what they have read in the paper. It seems to me that people who go to concerts are rather more discerning.

I know if I'm in a play and you get the kind of audience you think are not perhaps ready to listen, I know that through sheer technique, I will make them. They might think, 'Oh, why's she gone so funny?' and I'll stop them, stamp on it, which is a very difficult thing. It mustn't be overworked, it mustn't be overused, and you mustn't be too proud of it, but sometimes you will say, 'No.' A friend of Peter Gill's always laughs about this and says, 'The reason you want to be on stage is that you can't bear being in an audience.' But you have to let the audience know, 'I am here for a reason, and you're not going to play around and be silly; you're going to listen.' Sometimes different little things can really arrest their attention, which is valid.

It all comes down to the same thing: if you want to be heard, then you will have to learn something that is usually called technique, and that's all there is to it. If you don't want to be heard, then I don't quite know what you are doing, I don't know what you're here for, have a lovely time by yourself. It's called a very rude word.

I suppose when you think about it, being brought up with television,
which is very sort of one-to-one…

Yes, but really when you think about it, it's so stupid. Speaking to you here I can speak at this volume, but if you were at the back of the Globe, I'd have to speak in a different way. It's just bloody common sense, isn't it? But so much of where you start from in acting, and in everything else, is common sense and simplicity. You can't stand in the wings saying, 'I'm going to be great tonight.' I mean, can you imagine anything worse? We all know what we have to do, but some people put a very damaging mystique about the fundamentals of acting. There are a lot of people who would appear to be non-starters with things wrong with them, but who have made themselves better actors. There are quite a few who have really made themselves, by the force of their work and their will, into much better actors. Whereas people with more obvious equipment to start with haven't, because they've been a bit lazier.

JOHN GIELGUD

It was not possible to arrange a time for John Gielgud to be interviewed, but he returned the list of questions that were put at these interviews with notes handwritten against them, in April 1986. These were his responses:

Were you influenced by a particular teacher, director or colleague at an early stage in your career?

Claude Rains, Noël Coward, Theodor Komisarjevsky, Michel St Denis, Peter Brook, Harley Granville Barker.

What other colleagues do you admire, or have been influenced by?

Sybil Thorndike, Edith Evans, Ralph Richardson, Peggy Ashcroft, Leon Quartermaine.

What do you think is meant by good speaking? If an actor is speaking well, what is he doing?

Interpreting the text in appreciation of the kind of play concerned. Not indulging vocal excellence.

Who among your younger contemporaries do you think speaks well?

Ian McKellen, Judi Dench, Derek Jacobi, Robert Eddison, Michael Pennington, Dorothy Tutin.

Have you observed a change in speaking in the theatre in your lifetime?

Considerable, especially as regards the classics.

Would you approach the discipline of speaking a classical and a modern role in the same way? In short is good speaking absolute or variable?

(No answer given.)

What have been the influences that have changed speaking in the theatre?

Prevalence of the microphone. Fashion world developments.

If an actor is speaking badly, what is he doing?

Ignoring phrasing and punctuation.

Talking about Shakespeare, do you apply different rules to prose and verse?

No.

Are there any disciplines in the speaking of either that you would like to see generally applied?

Good speech should be expected from any experienced performer but differently controlled according to media – stage, screen, recording, TV, radio.

In verse, does end-stopping matter?

What about the caesura?

Feminine endings?

Rhyming couplets?

Broken lines?

(Against all these, Sir John has drawn a large question mark.)

How do you handle the beat of the iambic line? Do you ignore it and phrase for musicality and sense, trusting that by giving these their proper value the best result will be achieved?

Sometimes Shakespeare demands this.

What about vowels?

Of course.

Consonants?

Very important, especially at ends of words.

Breath?

Should not be noticeable.

Variation of tone?

Of course.

Audibility?

Essential.

Beauty of sound?

When necessary.

How do you reconcile the actor's personal need for expressiveness with the classical demands of the text?

Much depends upon rapport with partners and intentions of director.

Who, in your experience, could be imitated without being a bad influence?

One always starts by imitation of admired speakers, as in painting and music.

Who, other than acting colleagues, have influenced you with regard to speaking?

Early experience in radio. McKechnie. Lilian. Harrison.

Biographies

HARRY ANDREWS (1911–89)

Harry Andrews made his first appearance on stage at the Liverpool Playhouse in 1933, in *The Long Christmas Dinner*. From 1937 to 1938 he was with John Gielgud's company at the Queen's. He served with the Royal Artillery during WW2, reappearing on stage at the New Theatre with the Old Vic company from 1946 to 1949. Joined the company at Stratford from 1949, playing leading roles including Enobarbus, Buckingham, Kent, Claudius, and the title role in *Othello*. At the Old Vic in 1958, he played Henry VIII. In the 1960s he was at the Haymarket in *Ross* and later in *You Never Can Tell*, at the Phoenix he played Ekart in Brecht's *Baal*, and in 1971 the title role in Edward Bond's *Lear* at the Royal Court. His films included *The Red Beret, Ice-Cold in Alex, The Hill, Entertaining Mr. Sloane, Nicholas and Alexandra, The Nightcomers, The Ruling Class, Man of La Mancha, Theatre of Blood, Equus, The Prince and the Pauper, The Big Sleep, Death on the Nile, The Medusa Touch* and *Superman*.

GABRIELLE DAYE (1911–2005)

Gabrielle Daye's first stage appearance was in *The Dear Departed* at Rusholme Rep. She toured as Ruby Birtle in JB Priestley's *When We Are Married*, and later played the same part on BBC television. Her many other TV appearances included *Persuasion, I Didn't Know You Cared, All Creatures Great and Small*, the Plays for Today *The Pigeon Fancier* and *Sunset Across the Bay, Bleak House, Bless Me Father, Ever Decreasing Circles* and *A Very British Coup*. Her films included *Twilight Hour, Saints and Sinners, Little Big Shot, 10 Rillington Place* and *In Celebration*.

FABIA DRAKE (1904–90)

Fabia Drake made her first appearance on stage as a child, at the Court Theatre in 1913, as Tommy in *The Fairy Doll*; she also played Petruchio to Laurence Olivier's Kate at school. She studied at RADA, gaining the Vedrenne scholarship, and after many appearances in the West End, joined the Stratford-on-Avon Festival for a tour of the US and Canada, playing Lady Macbeth and Viola. She was in the company for the opening of the New Stratford Memorial Theatre in 1932, playing leading roles; and subsequently played Rosalind in *As You Like It* and the Princess in *Lady Precious Stream* in the West End. Her television appearances included playing Aunt Agatha in *The World of Wooster*, and the Countess of Midlothian in *The Pallisers*; and her many films included *Valmont, A Room With a View* and *Tam Lin*.

GWEN FFRANGCON-DAVIES (1891–1992)

Gwen Ffrangcon-Davies made her stage debut in 1911, as a singer as well as an actress. In 1924, she played Juliet opposite John Gielgud as Romeo. In 1938, she appeared with Ivor Novello in a production of *Henry V* at Drury Lane. In the same year she appeared as Mrs Manningham in the first production of *Gaslight* by Patrick Hamilton. She played Lady Macbeth for almost an entire year in 1942 opposite Gielgud's Macbeth. She retired from the stage after appearing in *Uncle Vanya* at the Royal Court in 1970, but continued to appear on radio and television. She was created a DBE in 1991, six months before her death at 101. Her films included *The Witches* (1966) and *The Devil Rides Out* (1968).

JOHN GIELGUD (1904–2000)

John Gielgud first came to prominence as a stage actor in classical roles at the Old Vic from 1929 to 1931, where his Richard II and Hamlet (which he eventually played over 500 times in six productions) were particularly acclaimed. His many successes included *Richard of Bordeaux, Romeo and Juliet* (in which he and Laurence Olivier alternated the parts of Mercutio and Romeo), *Three Sisters, The Cherry Orchard, Ivanov, Much Ado About Nothing, A Midsummer Night's Dream, The Winter's Tale*. He performed his one-man recital of Shakespeare extracts, *Ages of Man*, throughout the 1950s and 60s, and also recorded it. In later life, he appeared in modern plays including Albee's *Tiny Alice*, Alan Bennett's *Forty Years On*, Charles Wood's *Veterans*, David Storey's *Home* and Harold Pinter's *No Man's Land*, in which he appeared at the National Theatre and in the West End.

His other NT appearances included *Tartuffe, The Tempest, Julius Caesar, Volpone* and *Half Life.* He appeared in a great many films, from 1924 to 2000, and also became a noted stage director.

PETER GILL

Peter Gill began his career as an actor. In 1964 he became Assistant Director at the Royal Court and, in 1970, Associate Director. He was Founder Director of the Riverside Studios. He was Associate Director of the National Theatre 1980–97, and was Founding Director of the National Theatre Studio. His directing includes, for the National: *The Voysey Inheritance, Luther, Scenes from the Big Picture, Cardiff East, A Month in the Country, Don Juan, Much Ado About Nothing, Danton's Death, Major Barbara, Tales from Hollywood, Small Change, Kick for Touch, Antigone, Venice Preserv'd* and *Fool for Love.* For the Royal Court: *A Collier's Friday Night, The Local Stigmatic, The Ruffian on the Stair, A Provincial Life, The Soldier's Fortune, The Daughter-in-Law, The Widowing of Mrs Holroyd, Life Price, The Sleepers Den, Over Gardens Out, The Duchess of Malfi, Crete and Sergeant Pepper, The Merry-Go-Round, The Fool* and *Small Change.* For Riverside Studios: *The Cherry Orchard, The Changeling, Measure for Measure, Julius Caesar* and *Scrape off the Black.* For the RSC: *Twelfth Night, New England* and *A Patriot for Me.* Directing elsewhere includes *Gaslight* at the Old Vic, *Epitaph for George Dillon* at the Comedy; *Days of Wine and Roses* at the Donmar; *The Way of the World* at the Lyric, Hammersmith; *Uncle Vanya* for Field Day; *The York Realist* for English Touring Theatre; *Original Sin* for the Crucible, Sheffield; *Tongue of a Bird* and *Certain Young Men* at the Almeida and *Speed-the-Plow* at the New Ambassadors. His plays include *The Sleepers Den, Over Gardens Out, Small Change, Kick for Touch, In the Blue, Mean Tears, Cardiff East, Certain Young Men, Friendly Fire, The Look Across the Eyes, Lovely Evening, Original Sin* and *The York Realist.* Adaptations and versions: *A Provincial Life, The Merry-Go-Round, The Cherry Orchard, Touch and Go, As I Lay Dying* and *The Seagull.*

ALEC GUINNESS (1914–2000)

Alec Guinness studied for the stage at the Fay Compton Studio of Dramatic Art, and made his debut at the Albery Theatre in 1936, playing Osric in John Gielgud's production of *Hamlet*. In 1937 he played Aumerle in *Richard II* and Lorenzo in *The Merchant of Venice*, also directed by Gielgud. In 1938 he played Hamlet to acclaim on both sides of the Atlantic. He also appeared as Romeo in *Romeo and Juliet*, Andrew Aguecheek in *Twelfth Night*, Chorus in *Henry V*, and Ferdinand in *The Tempest*. In 1939 he adapted Dickens' *Great Expectations* for the stage, playing Herbert Pocket, as he also did in David Lean's 1946 film adaptation. During the war, he served in the Navy, returning to the Old Vic in 1946, to play Drugger in *The Alchemist*, the Fool in *King Lear*, DeGuiche in *Cyrano de Bergerac* and Richard II. He later appeared in T S Eliot's *The Cocktail Party*, Simon Gray's *Wise Child*, Alfred Jarry's *Ubu Roi* and Alan Bennett's *The Old Country*. On film, he was in *Kind Hearts and Coronets*, *The Lavender Hill Mob*, *The Ladykillers* and *The Man in the White Suit*; and in Lean's *Oliver Twist* and *Bridge on the River Kwai* (Academy Award), *Lawrence of Arabia*, *Doctor Zhivago* and *A Passage to India*; also *The Horse's Mouth*, *Tunes of Glory*, the title role in *Hitler: The Last Ten Days* and *Star Wars*. His regular TV appearances included playing George Smiley in *Tinker, Tailor, Soldier, Spy* and *Smiley's People*.

REX HARRISON (1908–90)

Rex Harrison first appeared on the stage in 1924 at Liverpool Repertory Theatre. During World War II he served in the RAF. In the West End, he appeared in Terence Rattigan's *French Without Tears*, Coward's *Design for Living*, Eliot's *The Cocktail Party*, *Bell, Book and Candle*, which he also directed, Shaw's *Heartbreak House*, Pirandello's *Enrico IV*, Lonsdale's *Aren't We All?* and J M Barrie's *The Admirable Crichton*. At the Royal Court, he was in *Platonov* and *August for the People*. He was best known for his portrayal of Professor Higgins in the musical *My Fair Lady*, on stage and film. His other films included *Doctor Dolittle*, *Cleopatra*, *Staircase*, *The Agony and the Ecstasy* and *Blithe Spirit*.

PATRICIA HAYES (1910-98)

Patricia Hayes made her first appearance on stage at the Court Theatre in 1921, in *The Great Big World*. After studying at RADA, where she gained the Bancroft Gold Medal, she appeared with the Oxford Players under J B Fagan, and with the Jevan Brandon-Thomas company at Edinburgh, Glasgow and Stratford. She made many appearances in the West End, her biggest success being as Ruby Birtle in the first production of J B Priestley's *When We Are Married*. She featured in many TV comedy shows and films between 1940 and 1996, including *Hancock's Half Hour*, *The Arthur Askey Show*, *The Benny Hill Show*, *Till Death Us Do Part*, *The Neverending Story* and *A Fish Called Wanda*. Her most famous TV appearance was in the title role of the 1971 TV play *Edna, the Inebriate Woman* for which she won a BAFTA.

MICHAEL HORDERN (1911-95)

Michael Hordern made his first appearance on the professional stage at the People's Palace in 1937, as Lodovico in *Othello*. After serving in the Navy in World War II, returned to the stage at the Intimate Theatre, Palmers Green, as Helmer in *A Doll's House*. His theatre work included seasons at the Shakespeare Memorial Theatre, Stratford, Old Vic (including *King Lear*, which visited from Nottingham Playhouse), Royal Shakespeare Company, and in the West End. For the National Theatre, he was in *Jumpers*, *Richard II*, *The Cherry Orchard* and *The Rivals*. His many films included *El Cid*, *Cleopatra*, *The Spy Who Came in from the Cold*, *The Slipper and the Rose*, *Futtocks End* and *The Missionary*.

ATHENE SEYLER (1889-1990)

Athene Seyler made her first appearance on stage at the Kingsway Theatre in 1909 as Pamela Grey in *The Truants*, and appeared in innumerable plays in the West End until the 1960s. With Stephen Haggard she wrote *The Craft of Comedy* published in 1944. She was elected president of RADA in 1950, the first former pupil to become its president. Her film and television career lasted into the 1960s, and included roles in *Night of the Demon* and *The Avengers*. She was also a regular cast member in screen adaptations of Charles Dickens novels. She continued making appearances well into the 1980s, memorably as a guest of Terry Wogan on his chat show. To celebrate her 101st birthday, and the republication of *The Craft of Comedy* in 1990, she appeared in a Platform discussion at the National Theatre.

ROBERT STEPHENS (1931–95)

Robert Stephens made his first London stage appearance in *The Crucible* at the Royal Court. His other work there included *Epitaph for George Dillon*, *Look after Lulu* and *The Kitchen*. His other work in London included *The Entertainer*, *Private Lives*, *Ghosts*, *The Seagull*, *Hamlet* and *Zoo Story*. For the NT his work included, at the Old Vic: *Hamlet*, *Saint Joan*, *The Recruiting Officer*, *Andorra*, *Play*, *The Royal Hunt of the Sun*, *Hay Fever*, *Much Ado About Nothing*, *Armstrong's Last Goodnight*, *Trelawny of the Wells*, *Black Comedy*, *The Dance of Death*, *Three Sisters*, *As You Like It*, *Tartuffe*, *The Beaux' Stratagem* and *Hedda Gabler*; on the South Bank: *The Cherry Orchard*, *The Double Dealer*, *A Midsummer Night's Dream*, *Inner Voices* and *The Mysteries*. For the RSC, he played Falstaff in 1993, winning the Olivier Award for Best Actor.

MADOLINE THOMAS (1891–1990)

Madoline Thomas spent six years with the RSC. At the Royal Court, she appeared in *Three Sisters*, *Marya*, *Uncle Vanya*, and *Sleepers Den*. At the National Theatre, she was in *Tales from the Vienna Woods*, *Strife*, *The Country Wife*, *The Guardsman* and *Uncle Vanya*. Her many TV appearances included *When the Boat Comes In*, *Mrs Palfrey at the Claremont*, *Just William*, *Shoestring*, *The Two Ronnies* and *Sons and Lovers*. Her films included *The Girl of the Canal*, *The Picture of Dorian Gray*, *Something to Hide* and *Burke and Hare*.

MARGARET TYZACK

Margaret Tyzack trained at RADA. Her work in theatre includes, at the National: *Southwark Fair*, *His Girl Friday*, *Tartuffe* and *Who's Afraid of Virginia Woolf?*, for which she won an Olivier Award for Best Actress in a Revival. For the RSC: *The Family Reunion, Summerfolk, Coriolanus, Titus Andronicus, Julius Caesar* and *The Lower Depths*; and *As You Desire Me, Talking Heads, Indian Ink, An Inspector Calls, The Importance of Being Earnest, Lettice and Lovage* (also on Broadway, Tony Award for Best Actress) and *Vivat! Vivat Regina!* in the West End. Margaret Tyzack won the Variety Club of Great Britain Stage Actress of the Year in 1987. Her work in TV includes *Doc Martin, Rosemary and Thyme, Wallis and Edward, Midsomer Murders, Heartbeat, Dalziel and Pascoe, The First Churchills* (BAFTA Best Actress), *Our Mutual Friend, An Inspector Calls, I Claudius* and *The Forsyte Saga*. Her films include *Match Point, Bright Young Things, Mrs Dalloway, A Clockwork Orange, 2001: A Space Odyssey* and *Behind the Mask*.

.